THEATRICAL MAKEUP

In many theatrical productions, it falls to the performers to apply their own makeup, with minimal or no instruction. *Theatrical Makeup* clearly and concisely explains the basics of theatrical makeup techniques to allow stage actors to put their best face forward! You will gain understanding of the physiology of the human face and, using cream-based makeup, as well as commercial cosmetics, learn how to contour it to suit your character with the use of highlight and shadow. Hundreds of full color images and step-by-step instructions illustrate how to visually manipulate bone structure and apparent age, apply simple facial hair and wounds, and create glamorous and natural stage makeup. Also covered are the tools you will need to apply your own makeup, along with critical health and hygiene tips.

- Makeup is applied to a diverse group of models, incorporating a variety of ages and ethnicities
- Thoroughly covers application techniques for makeup displayed under theatrical lighting
- Also included is a detailed discussion of how to use makeup to change the perception of gender or age, working with common skin textures and abnormalities, and creating historical makeup looks
- A companion website, www.focalpress.com/cw/sobel, hosts application videos for even more detailed instructions

Sharon Sobel has taught Stage Makeup at the college level since 1990, with 21 of those years at the University of Nebraska at Omaha. She has taught Stage Makeup at the college level since 1990. She has lead multiple KCACTF workshops in makeup design and application and served as guest respondent for student makeup designs. She has designed and draped costumes and served as advisor for makeup for over 100 productions and is a member of United Scenic Artists of America. She is also a recipient of the Kennedy Center American College Theatre Festival Gold Medallion. Sharon is the author of *Draping Period Costumes: Classical Greek to Victorian*, published by Focal Press.

THEATRICAL MAKEUP

Basic Application Techniques

Sharon Sobel

Routledge
Taylor & Francis Group

LONDON AND NEW YORK

First published 2016 by Focal Press

Published 2016 by Routledge
52 Vanderbilt Avenue, New York, NY 10017
2 Park Square, Milton Park, Abingdon, Oxon OX14 4RN

Routledge is an imprint of the Taylor & Francis Group, an informa business

Library of Congress Cataloging-in Publication Data
Library of Congress Cataloging in Publication Data
Sobel, Sharon, 1959–

 Theatrical makeup : basic application techniques / Sharon
 Sobel. pages cm
 Includes index.
 1. Theatrical makeup—Handbooks, manuals, etc. I. Titl
 PN2068.S63 2015
 792.02′7—dc23
 2014044617

ISBN: 978-1-138-79876-2 (pbk)
ISBN: 978-1-138-89882-0 (hbk)
ISBN: 978-1-315-75650-9 (ebk)

Typeset in Berkeley and Helvetica
By Florence Production Ltd, Stoodleigh, Devon, UK

All photography by Sharon Sobel

Dedicated to the memory of my dear brother Jonathan,
who made everyone he touched more beautiful.

CONTENTS

ACKNOWLEDGMENTS

I owe a great deal of thanks to a good many people, without whom this book would not have happened:

Avery Mazor, Department of Art and Art History, University of Nebraska at Omaha (UNO) for his generosity of time, energy, facilities, equipment, and spirit. Kyle Christianson, Student Worker in the UNO Graphic Design Studio, who saved me from the perils of technology.

Also at UNO, Dean of the College of Communication, Fine Arts, and Media, Dr. Gail Baker, and Chair of the Department of Theatre, D. Scott Glasser, for enthusiastically supporting my assigned time to complete this book.

Dear friends, Rob Urbinati, who took the time to teach me the joys of *The Elements of Style*, and Nick Newman, for all of his encouragement and shopping trips.

At Focal Press: my brilliant Acquisitions Editor, Stacey Walker, and my wonderful Editorial Project Manager, Meagan White. Thanks, too, to my technical editor, Angela Bacarisse for her great suggestions.

My beautiful and patient models, Ankita Ashrit, Maggie Fisher, Angela Horchem, Manuela Stephanie Lopez , Nick Newman, Andy Prescott, Jessica Rogers, Amy Fae Schweid, Emilio Sotelo, Dennis Stessman, Devin Tumpkin, Charleen J. B. Willoughby, and Ryann Woods.

Mallory Maria Prucha, of whom I am so proud, for her beautiful and professional illustrations.

Charles V. Fisher, of whom I am also very proud, for his beautiful and professional makeup worksheets.

My makeup students over the years who have taught me much.

My loving mother, Eileen, and sister, Martha, who are always there encouraging me.

Why another makeup book?

In most theatre situations, the performers are responsible for providing and applying their own makeup. There are some cases in which a makeup designer/artist will train the performers in a specific style (perhaps for a chorus of munchkins or flying monkeys in *The Wizard of Oz*) and provide specialty makeup. In many opera companies, a staff or contracted makeup artist will design and apply the makeup for the singers. But in realistic theatre productions (which are, arguably, the majority of contemporary performances) the performer is left to his or her own devices. Some performers have had makeup training in college, either through a course or in a workshop prior to a production. Those who have not are at a disadvantage.

I have been teaching theatrical makeup at the undergraduate level for 25 years. My students are attentive and hungry to learn. During every class meeting, proper makeup application techniques are demonstrated. Yet over and over these same dedicated students have difficulty replicating what they have been shown. One reason for this lack of retention is that few makeup texts demonstrate, step-by-step, the proper placement and blending of highlight and shadow.

Theatrical Makeup: Basic Application Techniques provides a reference for students and performers to use when applying their makeup. The primary focus of this book is on how to use highlight and shadow to contour the face for greater visibility and dimensionality under theatrical lighting. Additional topics include altering the natural shape of the face as a character device or to change the perception of one's age or gender, common skin textures and abnormalities, and historical makeups.

Theatrical Makeup: Basic Application Techniques demonstrates the basics, which is what most performers need to know. Animal and fantasy makeups will not be covered, neither will the casting of three-dimensional prosthetics; those are usually the responsibility of a makeup designer, not each individual actor. If the reader is interested in advancing beyond what is presented here, those more complex techniques are addressed in other, more comprehensive, makeup texts.

1

TOOLS AND MATERIALS

Two types of makeup are used in theatre productions: traditional theatrical makeup and cosmetics.

Traditional theatrical makeup, which can be bought at such places as a costume rental shop or novelty store, comes in several forms, the two most popular being cream (soft and moist) and pancake (dry). Cream makeup is ready to apply directly from the container. Pancake makeup requires water to activate it before it can be used. When using a cream foundation, cream highlight and shadow are used for contouring. Either a cream or powder color is used for cheek blush. When using a pancake foundation, either cream highlight and shadow, or powder shadow alone can be used for contouring. Traditional theatrical makeup continues to be used on larger stages where heavier coverage and stronger definition are required. Theatrical cream highlight and shadow are also necessary when applying age makeup or changing your features to any great degree. Brands of theatrical makeup include Ben Nye, Graftobian, Kryolan, and Mehron.

Cosmetics, worn by many women on a daily basis, are also used frequently in theatre, especially in smaller venues. But even on large Broadway stages and in many opera companies, some performers are wearing cosmetics. Liquid and cream foundation, and shadow or bronzing

A VARIETY OF LIQUID BASES AND CONTOURING POWDERS

powder for contouring, are readily available at cosmetics counters in department stores (Clinique, Estee Lauder, MAC, etc.) and in the cosmetic sections of health and beauty stores (Almay, Cover Girl, Maybelline, etc.)

If you have chosen theatrical makeup, you can either purchase a complete kit, which certain theatrical makeup manufacturers market to students and actors, or the following individual items:

- Foundation (discussed in Chapter 3)
- Cream highlight (discussed in Chapter 4)
- Cream shadow (discussed in Chapter 4)
- Cream or powder cheek color (discussed in Chapter 5)
- Lip color (discussed in Chapter 5)
- Lip-liner pencil (discussed in Chapter 5)
- Eyeliner pencil in brown or black, depending on the darkness of your hair or wig
- Setting powder
- Flat brushes for application of cream contouring. A 7/16-inch or 1/2-inch wide brush, which some brands refer to as size 12, is the ideal size for contouring bone structure
- Velour or velvet powder puff
- Stipple sponge

A VARIETY OF THEATRICAL FOUNDATIONS, HIGHLIGHTS, AND SHADOWS

BASIC THEATRICAL MAKEUP NEEDS

PALETTES FOR MIXING

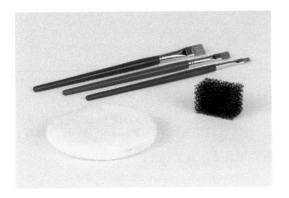

APPLICATION TOOLS

BASIC COSMETIC NEEDS

- You may also purchase a palette for mixing base and contouring colors. The palette can be any one of a variety of things: a professional makeup palette, an artist's painting palette, a white ceramic tile, or even a white or clear lid from a plastic container. Be sure it is clean and sanitized.

If you have chosen cosmetics, you will need to purchase the following individual items:

- Liquid foundation (discussed in Chapter 3)
- Primer (can be useful in very small, close venues)
- Concealer (discussed in Chapter 3)
- Setting powder (discussed in Chapter 4)
- Shadow or bronzing powder (discussed in Chapter 4)

- Neutral eye-shadow in dark and light shades (discussed in Chapter 5)
- Blush (discussed in Chapter 5)
- Lip color (discussed in Chapter 5)
- Lip-liner pencil (discussed in Chapter 5)
- Eyeliner pencil in brown or black, depending on the darkness of your hair or wig

For all types of makeup, you will need to purchase:

- Mascara, if you are a woman, or a man playing a woman, or a man performing in a very large venue
- Latex-free application sponges, which can be either wedge-shaped, or round and flat
- Large, rounded brushes for application of powder shadow and blush

SUPPLIES AVAILABLE AT A HEALTH AND BEAUTY RETAILER

- Smaller sized flat brushes for eyes, lips, etc. (¼-inch and ⅜-inch are useful sizes)

- Liner pencil sharpener

- Headband or hair clips

- Makeup remover in either liquid, cream, or towelette form, or baby towelettes (make sure makeup remover is alcohol-free so you don't dry out your skin)

- Facial cleanser

- Moisturizer

- Toner, if that is part of your regular cleansing regimen

- A carrying case with multiple drawers and compartments: some are made specifically for makeup and can be found in cosmetic departments, but a fishing tackle box is also effective

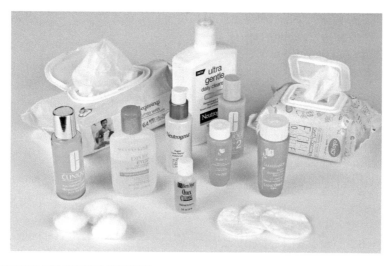

ADDITIONAL PRODUCTS FOR MAKEUP REMOVAL

CASES FOR STORING AND TRANSPORTING YOUR MAKEUP

TACKLE AND ART BOXES CAN ALSO BE USED

NOTE: NEVER STORE YOUR MAKEUP IN ANY LOCATION THAT IS NOT TEMPERATURE CONTROLLED; FREEZING AND HIGH TEMPERATURES WILL DAMAGE IT.

2

SAFETY AND HYGIENE

Test Makeup Before You Use It

In order for makeup to be sold legally, it must be tested for safety; however, certain people may have an allergic reaction. If you are using makeup for the first time, test it to make sure you are not allergic to it before applying it to your whole face. First apply it on the inside of your wrist; allow some time to see if there is a reaction. Next try it on your jawline and wait for a reaction. Finally, try it near your eyes, nose and mouth.

In some cases, red makeup may cause an allergic reaction if applied near the eyes. If you are prone to allergic reactions, do not apply makeup with red pigment near your eyes.

If you have any concerns about using theatrical or street makeup, first check with a licensed dermatologist.

Avoiding Infection

In the makeup room, safety and hygiene are of utmost importance. Actors often apply their makeup in close quarters, in a rush, and various infections can be spread. Pay attention to the following rules.

Do Not Share Your Makeup or Application Tools

Bacteria can pass from the face—particularly around the eyes, nose, and mouth—to a brush, then to a pan of makeup, and then to someone else's face. Because professional makeup artists use the same foundation and shadows on multiple performers, they are meticulous about cleaning their makeup and tools with an antibacterial solution after each performer. If you are using your own makeup, don't take a chance. You may be tempted to help a fellow actor in need, but you will be doing more harm than good by sharing germs.

Keep Your Tools Clean

Even if you are not sharing your makeup or tools, you could be re-infecting yourself with your own bacteria. Wash your brushes with an anti-bacterial soap or brush-cleansing solution after each application. Smooth the bristles back into shape to dry. Always discard the latex-free sponge when you finish your application.

Wash Your Hands and Face Before Applying Makeup

If there are bacteria on your hands you can transfer it to your face. Also wash your hands after applying makeup so you don't dirty your costume and hand props.

Proper Facial Cleansing After Makeup Removal

Theatrical makeup is only appropriate for use in the theatre. After the performance you need to remove your makeup. Continuing to wear theatrical makeup after the performance can lead to dermatological problems.

First, use a makeup remover. It might come in a liquid form, a cream form, or as a pre-moistened towelette. Baby wipes are also effective because they are very mild. After removing all visible makeup, wash your face with a mild soap or facial cleanser. Next, use a toner or cool water to close your pores. Finally, use an oil-free moisturizer.

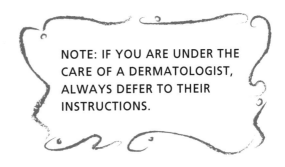

NOTE: IF YOU ARE UNDER THE CARE OF A DERMATOLOGIST, ALWAYS DEFER TO THEIR INSTRUCTIONS.

3

FOUNDATION

Why Use Foundation?

There are several reasons for wearing foundation while on stage. One reason is to alter your natural skin tone. You might do this to portray someone of a different age, someone who is ill or is healthier than you are, someone who has spent more or less time in the sun or other natural elements, or someone who is of a different ethnic background. You might just be very pale and wish to avoid reflecting too much light on stage. Foundation can also help to even out uneven skin tones, including ruddiness, acne, or sun damage.

Another reason to use makeup in general on stage is that strong theatrical lighting can cause your features to appear flat. Makeup, specifically highlight and shadow used for contouring, will restore the appearance of three-dimensionality. If you are using makeup for this reason, you must apply foundation before applying the highlights and shadows that define the features. The base coat of foundation is a necessary under-layer that helps when blending for a smooth and natural look.

Preparing the Face

When applying foundation your skin should be clean. Do not wear street makeup unless you are using an undercoat of hypoallergenic makeup, which is discussed below. Men should be clean-shaven unless their own facial hair is being used as part of the makeup design. Use either toner or cool water to close your pores. Apply an oil-free moisturizer before the makeup, leaving enough time for it to soak in. Also make sure that your hands are clean before applying your makeup. Use anti-bacterial soap or hand sanitizer.

If you have acne or skin allergies, check with a dermatologist before using theatrical makeup. You may want to apply a hypoallergenic

foundation before the theatrical foundation. If you have any fresh, unhealed facial piercings, which is not a smart choice for an actor, avoid those areas. Apply an anti-bacterial ointment to those areas for safety. If you sweat profusely, you may prepare your face with a sweat-blocker, which is sold by the major theatrical makeup manufacturers.

Choosing the Right Foundation

Depending on whether you are performing in a small or large theatre, or whether you want to look more natural or theatrically stylized, you might choose between a liquid foundation (cosmetic) and a heavier, cream-based foundation (theatrical). If you are responsible for providing your own makeup, it is a good idea to check with the costume or makeup designer for his or her preference. If there is no costume or makeup designer, try to be consistent with the other actors in your production.

Dry or pancake foundation is used less frequently than liquid and cream foundation. It is often used for body makeup or for performers with extremely oily skin or who sweat a lot.

Choosing a foundation color will depend on the character you are playing. For a basic corrective (your own age, ethnicity, looking your healthy best) you will choose a color close to your own skin tone, unless you are extremely pale. In that case you may need a foundation that is a little darker.

Most theatrical makeup companies now carry an assortment of foundation colors for an assortment of ethnic backgrounds. When testing for the correct color, try the foundation on your face after you have tested it for a reaction as described in Chapter 2. Do not test for color on your hand because your hand will tend to be darker, or even a different tone (i.e., yellower or redder) than your face.

THE FOUNDATION ON THE LEFT IS THE CLOSEST TO THE ACTOR'S NATURAL SKIN TONE. Model, Andrew Prescott

If you can't find the exact color foundation you need, you can blend two together, either on a palette or directly on your face.

Application of Theatrical Foundation

When using a cream-based foundation, use your middle finger to dot the makeup onto your face leaving spaces in between. If you are blending two colors on your face, dot them on, alternately, at the same time.

To avoid the transfer of bacteria from your face to the makeup container, scoop out the amount you will need using a palette knife or the end of a makeup brush and place it on a palette or the back of your hand.

BLENDING TWO FOUNDATION COLORS ON A PALETTE

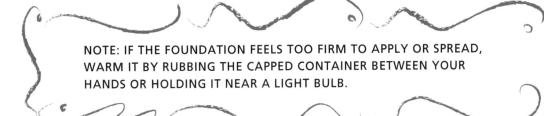

After applying the foundation, use a latex-free sponge to smooth the makeup across your face, covering every part of it. Do not rub the makeup into your pores. Glide the makeup just up to your hairline, out to the beginning of your ears and down past your jawline onto your neck. Remember to apply makeup around your eyes. Depending on whether or not you neck is paler or redder than your face, you can either fade out the foundation or continue it down to the base of your neck. Take into consideration the height or depth of the neckline of the costume you will be wearing, so you do not dirty it with makeup from your neck.

Work towards a smooth, even finish with no visible edge. The intention is to create a seamless coverage and to avoid the look of a mask.

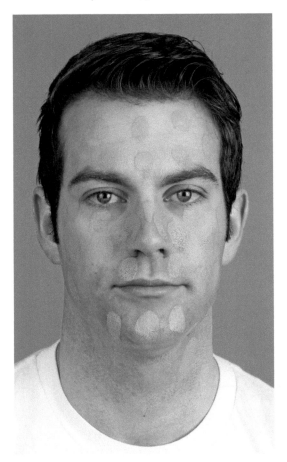

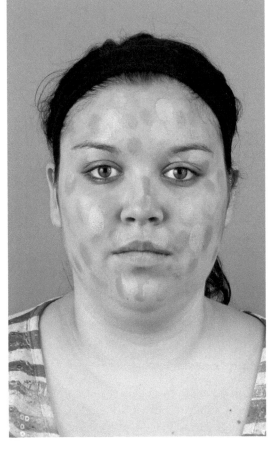

APPLY DOTS OF MAKEUP TO YOUR FACE USING YOUR FINGERTIPS

BLENDING TWO FOUNDATION COLORS ON YOUR FACE.
Model, Manuela Stephanie Lopez

CREAM FOUNDATION APPLIED

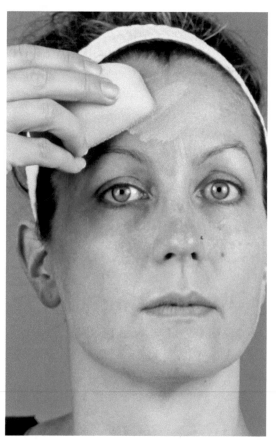

PANCAKE MAKEUP APPLICATION. Model, Angela Horchem

If you are using a dry pancake foundation, wet your application sponge with fresh, lukewarm water and squeeze out most, but not all, of the water. Rub it against the dry makeup to liquefy it; glide it across the face without grinding it into your pores. Repeat until you have a smooth, even finish.

Using Concealer

You may want to cover dark spots or areas (moles, birthmarks, blemishes, etc.) Many people have dark circles under their eyes that can make them look tired or older than they are or want to appear. To cover a dark area you must apply makeup that is lighter than the foundation you

have chosen. Your highlight color (see Chapter 4) often works best.

If you have dark circles under your eyes they will very likely have a purplish tone to them. The opposite of purple on the color wheel is yellow, therefore, mix some yellow in to your concealer. This will help to neutralize the purple tone.

NOTE: TO HIDE DARK AREAS YOU MUST USE A COLOR THAT IS LIGHTER THAN YOUR SKIN TONE.

COLOR WHEEL

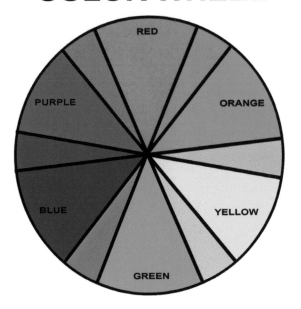

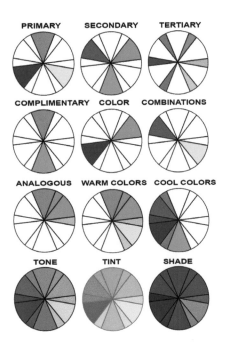

THE COLOR WHEEL. ILLUSTRATION BY MALLORY MARIA PRUCHA

If you are concealing acne, rosacea, or ruddiness, those skin conditions have a red tone; add a small amount of green, which is the opposite of red, to your concealer.

Use a brush to apply and smooth out the lighter color. Then dot on some of the foundation and blend it out beyond the edges of the dark spot, using a latex-free sponge.

GREEN AND YELLOW BLENDED INTO HIGHLIGHT

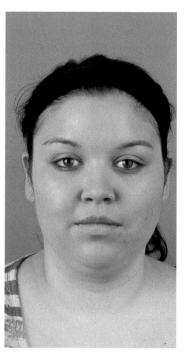

YELLOW-TINTED HIGHLIGHT USED AS CONCEALER

CONCEALER BLENDED

BEFORE CONCEALER

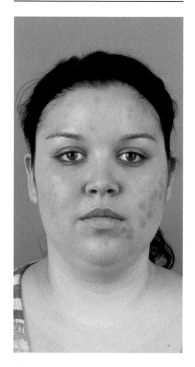

GREEN-TINTED HIGHLIGHT USED AS CONCEALER

CONCEALER BLENDED OUT

FOUNDATION OVER CONCEALER

Application of Cosmetics Foundation and Concealer

Your face should be clean and prepared in the same manner as you would for theatrical makeup. Apply concealer first; you can buy yellow- or green-tinted concealer at a health and beauty retailer. Using either a flat brush or an applicator if one comes with it, smooth out the edges.

Pour or pump some of the liquid foundation into your hand or onto a palette. Dot it on to your face with your finger and spread it lightly across your face with a latex-free sponge in the same manner as you would for theatrical makeup.

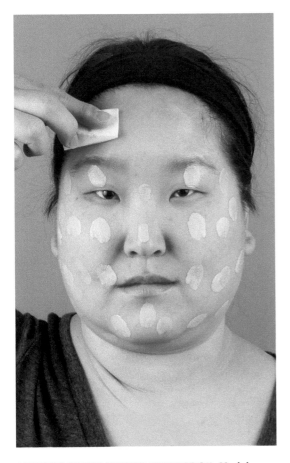

APPLYING STREET MAKEUP FOUNDATION. Model, Jessica Rogers

Setting the Cosmetic Foundation with Powder

Set your cosmetic foundation with powder before contouring. Set your theatrical foundation with powder after contouring and any other technique that uses cream makeup.

Pressed setting powder is usually sold with a velour or velvet application pad. Rub the pad on the powder and then press it evenly all over your face.

When using a loose powder, press the powder puff into the loose powder. Fold the powder puff together and rub the powder in. Open the puff and flick the bottom, loosening the powder. Press the powder into the foundation on your face. If the powder looks cakey, go over the spot, lifting some off and redistributing it. To loosen more powder, flick the back of the puff again. Once you have powder on your entire face, wet a latex-free cosmetic sponge. Wring all the water from the sponge and press it over the powder so that it seems to disappear.

NOTE: WHEN YOU ARE DONE APPLYING YOUR MAKEUP, THROW YOUR APPLICATION SPONGE AWAY—DO NOT SAVE IT. IT CAN BECOME A BREEDING GROUND FOR BACTERIA.

4

CONTOURING

Why Contouring is Needed

Strong theatrical lighting can make your features look flat and hard to distinguish. Wearing makeup can restore the appearance of three-dimensionality. To do that, utilize the same tools as an artist—highlight and shadow. An artist uses lighter colors to make things appear as if they are coming towards you, and darker colors to make things recede.

When discussing highlight and shadow an artist refers to the value scale; the darkest colors have a value of 100 (percentage of pigment), the lightest colors have a value of 0 (percentage of pigment).

Contouring Using Theatrical Cream Makeup

When using theatrical cream or pancake foundation, cream highlight (lighter than your foundation) is painted on the areas that protrude (cheekbones, jawline, etc.) Cream shadow (darker than your foundation) is painted on areas that recede (sides of the nose, indentations under the cheekbones, etc.). An area of foundation is left in between the areas of highlight and shadow. This neutral area will help give a soft edge to the contouring when blending the highlight and shadow. If you place the highlight and shadow too close together, without leaving enough room to blend the edges into the base tone of the foundation, you will create a hard or sharp edge. This technique can be used to create wrinkles and folds when applying makeup for middle and old age, but is not appropriate for regular contouring.

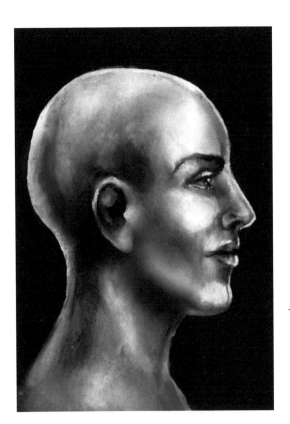

DRAWING BY MALLORY MARIA PRUCHA

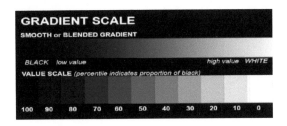

ILLUSTRATION BY MALLORY MARIA PRUCHA

NOTE: FOR NORMAL CONTOURING, ALWAYS LEAVE AN AREA OF FOUNDATION BETWEEN HIGHLIGHT AND SHADOW.

Choosing Your Highlight and Shadow Colors

The highlight color should be several shades lighter than the foundation. If you have extremely pale skin, you might choose a white or off-white highlight. If your skin is olive or darker (especially if you are primarily of African descent) you will choose a beige or tan highlight. Your shadow color should be several shades darker than your foundation, and in the brown range. Do not use black as a shadow color, even if your skin tone is very dark. Instead, try blending a small amount of dark purple or blue into a dark brown shadow color.

If you have bought a complete student makeup kit, appropriate highlight and shadow colors are included. If you buy individual items, ask the salesperson to help you choose. Hopefully they will have had training in theatrical makeup, or at least have a good eye and sense of color.

Contouring the Forehead

While looking in the mirror, run your fingers over your forehead and feel where it protrudes and where it recedes. There is an upper ridge below your hairline and a lower ridge just above your eyebrows. These ridges tend to be more prominent on men than on women, although, there are always exceptions.

Run your fingers along the sides of your forehead; these flat, receding planes are the temples.

Using the flat side of your flat, wide brush (size 12 or 7/16-inch), apply a wide swath of highlight

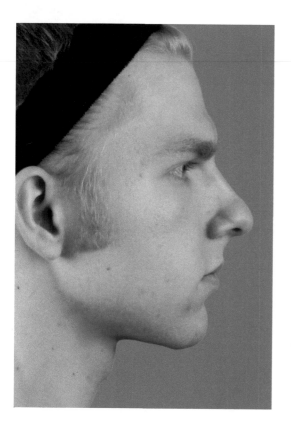

PROMINENT FOREHEAD RIDGES ON MAN. Model, Denis Stessman

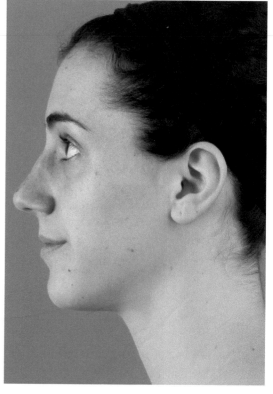

SHALLOWER FOREHEAD RIDGES ON WOMAN. Model, Amy Fae Schweid

APPLYING THE HIGHLIGHT TO THE FOREHEAD

APPLYING THE SHADOW BETWEEN THE FOREHEAD RIDGES

19

to the upper and lower ridges of the forehead, beginning and ending before you reach the temples. These ridges will be shaped somewhat like an archery bow, dipping down in the center. Don't use so much that it looks thick; use only enough that you can see it.

> NOTE: YOU CAN APPLY ALL OF YOUR HIGHLIGHTS AT ONCE AND THEN ALL OF YOUR SHADOWS AT ONCE. FOR DEMONSTRATION PURPOSES WE WILL BE WORKING FEATURE BY FEATURE.

Wipe the highlight off of your brush until it is clean. Do this every time you change makeup colors. Pick up a little bit of your shadow color and apply a wide swath of it to the recessed area between the upper and lower ridges of the forehead. This swath of makeup should also be shaped somewhat like an archery bow. Notice that there is space in between the highlight and shadow.

> NOTE: ALWAYS WIPE OFF YOUR BRUSH WHEN SWITCHING FROM HIGHLIGHT TO SHADOW AND BACK.

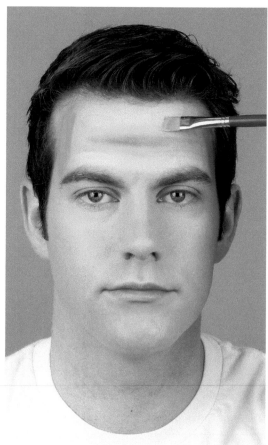

APPLYING THE SHADOW TO THE TEMPLES

BLENDING THE HIGHLIGHT

The temples are relatively flat planes of the face; the shape of the shadow will be rather wide. Paint some shadow (about two brushes wide) onto your temples in a vertical direction.

Wipe the shadow off of your brush until it is clean. Using your brush, follow the highlights along the outer edges *in the direction in which you applied it*. Use the brush to pick up and remove some of the highlight along the edges. You may need to wipe off your brush. Leave the thickest amount of highlight in the center of the swath. This is *blending*. Good blending is one of the most important things you need to know in order to apply your makeup well.

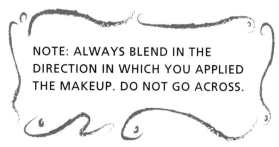

NOTE: ALWAYS BLEND IN THE DIRECTION IN WHICH YOU APPLIED THE MAKEUP. DO NOT GO ACROSS.

Use the same technique to blend out the shadow. Be very careful that the highlight and the shadow do not meet. Leave an area of base tone in between the two when contouring.

Now you know the basic technique of using highlight and shadow to contour, you can move on to the other areas of the face.

BLENDED HIGHLIGHT AND SHADOW

NOTE: AFTER BLENDING, MOVE
BACK FROM YOUR MIRROR A FEW
FEET TO LOOK AT YOUR MAKEUP.
REMEMBER THAT YOU ARE
APPLYING MAKEUP TO BE SEEN
FROM FAR AWAY, NOT UP CLOSE.

Contouring the Cheekbones

In the same way you examined the forehead, run your fingers over your cheekbones and feel where they protrude and where they sink in. Notice that the cheekbones begin just in front of the top of

the ear and angle downward as they move towards the pads of the cheeks. The cheekbones stop directly under the outer corners of the eyes. There is a depression underneath the cheekbones, where you may be able to feel your upper molars.

Using the flat side of your wide, flat brush, apply a swath of highlight to the outer flat surface of the cheekbone. Start in front of the upper ear and slowly lift your brush as you angle down towards the pad of the cheek. This lifting motion will make the highlight fade out, in effect, blending it into the base tone.

Using the flat side of your wide brush, apply a swath of shadow below, and parallel to, your highlight. Leave an area of base tone in between.

21

APPLYING HIGHLIGHT TO THE CHEEKBONE

BLENDING THE CHEEKBONE

APPLYING SHADOW TO THE CHEEKBONE

Using the same technique as you did with your forehead, blend the highlights and then the shadows, making sure that the highlight and the shadow do not meet. Remember to blend the highlight and the shadow in the direction in which you applied them, never across or perpendicular.

BLENDED CHEEKBONE

Contouring the Jawline

Feel how your jawline begins in front of the bottom of your ear. It heads downward and then turns a corner, or curves, continuing on to the chin. Some people have a more prominent or angled corner to their jawline; some have a softer curve. Depending on your age and weight, you may have to try a little harder to find the bones of the jawline.

Using the flat side of your wide brush, apply a swath of highlight to the outer flat surface of the jawline. Start in front of the lower ear and work down. Either turn at the corner (if it is prominent) or curve around it. Slowly lift your brush as you head towards the chin.

Because the underside of the jawline faces down, you might need to use a hand mirror or ask a fellow performer to help you apply the shadow. The area of base tone you leave will be narrower and you will need to blend into a smaller area.

SHADOWING THE JAWLINE

HIGHLIGHTING THE JAWLINE

BLENDED JAWLINE

Contouring the Chin

There are many differently shaped chins. Some are rounded, some have clefts, some have dimples. Following are some examples of ways to contour a variety of chin shapes.

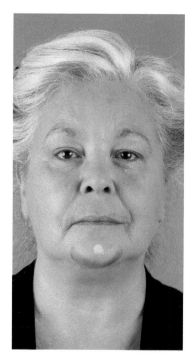

CONTOURING A ROUND CHIN. Model, Charleen J. B. Willoughby

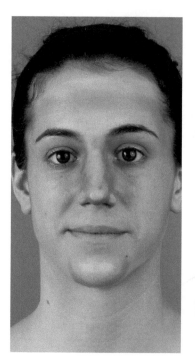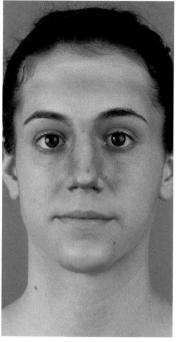

CONTOURING A SQUARE CHIN

Contouring the Nose

The nose has several distinct parts to it: the bridge, the tip, and the nares (the fleshy parts that surround the nostrils.) There are a variety of shapes, but when contouring, we can approach the three distinct parts of every nose similarly.

The bridge is a vertical, relatively cylindrical shape, and will be contoured as such. Using a medium flat brush, apply a swath of highlight from the top of the bridge, down until just before the tip.

Apply a swath of shadow on either side of the bridge of the nose, ending at the nare, leaving some room to blend.

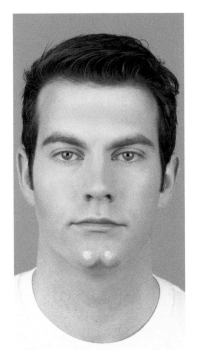

CONTOURING A CLEFT CHIN

HIGHLIGHTING THE BRIDGE OF THE NOSE

SHADOWING THE BRIDGE OF THE NOSE

25

If the nose is relatively straight and narrow, apply an arc of shadow at the end of the nose, under the tip.

Carefully blend the edges of your highlight and shadow.

SHADOW UNDER TIP OF THE NOSE

BLENDING THE BRIDGE OF THE NOSE

If the tip of the nose is rounded, you can stop at the point where it begins to swell outward. Then put a dot of highlight on the highest point of the nose.

Shadow and blend the bridge as previously described. Then apply shadow, in an arc shape, under the rounded tip of the nose. Leave an area of base tone between the dot of highlight and the arc of shadow.

Blend.

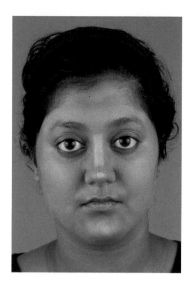

HIGHLIGHTING A NOSE WITH A ROUNDED TIP. Model, Ankita Ashrit

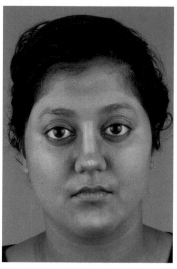

SHADOWING A NOSE WITH A ROUNDED TIP

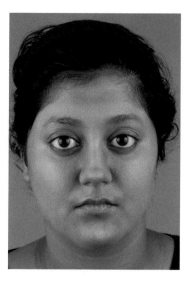

BLENDED HIGHLIGHT AND SHADOW

Contouring the Eyes

Contouring a woman's eyes and contouring a man's eyes need to be approached in different ways. Men are more likely to have a prominent lower brow bone protruding over their eyes; therefore, much of the upper lid may be hidden. The goal is to make as much of the upper lid visible as possible without "feminizing" the man's face (unless he is playing a woman.) Women tend to have more of the eyelid showing; therefore there is more room to contour.

For the woman, use a medium-sized brush to apply highlight to the brow bone under the eyebrow. Next, apply highlight to the center of the upper eyelid, starting at the eyelash and ending at the crease.

Blend out the edges of your highlights.

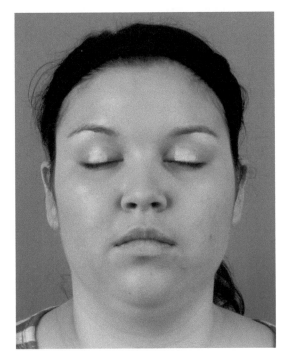

HIGHLIGHT APPLIED TO BROW BONE AND CENTER OF EYELID

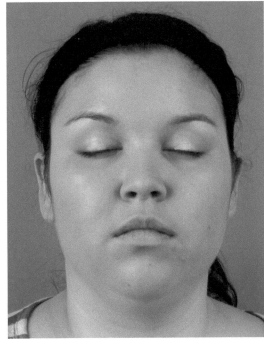

HIGHLIGHT BLENDED OUT TO BASE TONE

Apply shadow to the outer corners of the upper eyelid and in the crease above the lid. Make sure you leave a space between the highlight and the shadow.

Blend out the edges of your shadows. Make sure that you don't blend into your highlights.

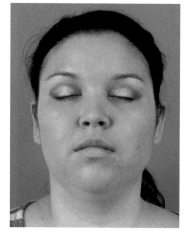

SHADOW APPLIED TO EYELID AND CREASE

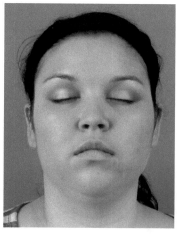

SHADOW BLENDED OUT TO BASE TONE

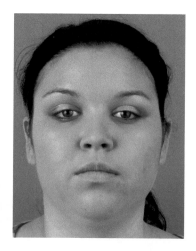

EYES CONTOURED WITH CREAM HIGHLIGHT AND SHADOW

Proper placement of highlight and shadow can help to give a more youthful appearance if that is desired.

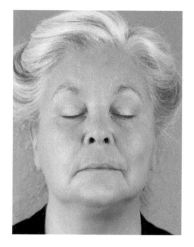

HIGHLIGHT APPLIED TO BROW BONE AND CENTER OF EYELID

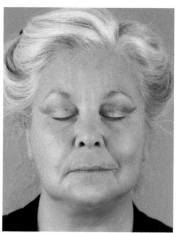

SHADOW APPLIED TO CREASE IN AN UPWARD CURVE

BLENDED HIGHLIGHT AND SHADOW

For the man, apply highlight along the front edge of the eyelid, right next to the lashes.

Blend the highlight towards the crease.

HIGHLIGHT APPLIED TO FRONT OF EYELID

HIGHLIGHT BLENDED

If you are a man or a woman of Asian descent it is likely that much of your eyelid will be hidden by the epicanthic fold. Your goal is to make as much of the lid visible as possible without westernizing your face.

Apply highlight along the front edge of the eyelid and blend it back towards the crease.

If you are a woman, or a man playing one, apply highlight just below the outer edge of the eyebrow and blend it out to base tone.

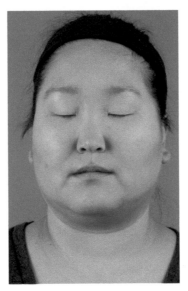

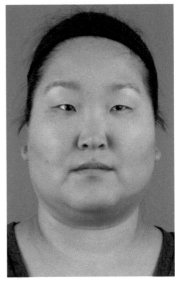

HIGHLIGHT APPLIED TO FRONT OF EYELID AND BLENDED

HIGHLIGHT APPLIED TO BROW BONE

Apply shadow to the inner corner of the eye, next to the bridge of the nose. Curve the shadow just onto the epicanthic fold. Do not apply shadow where the crease would be on a western eyelid, unless you want to westernize your eye.

Blend the highlight and shadow.

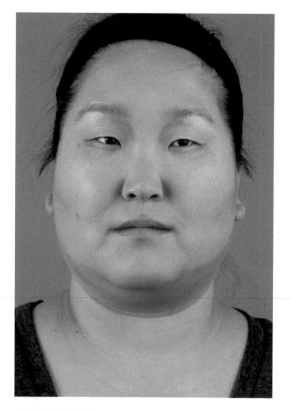

SHADOW AT THE INNER CORNER OF THE EYE

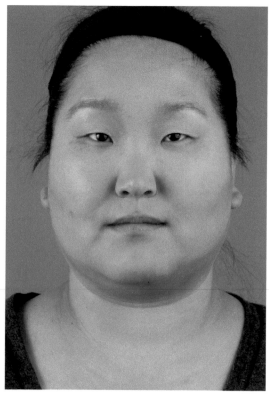

BLENDED HIGHLIGHT AND SHADOW

Setting the Makeup with Powder

At this point you have applied your theatrical foundation, highlight, and shadow. If this is the last of your cream makeup application, you need to set it now. If you will be applying cream rouge, rather than powder rouge, wait until after that to powder.

Theatrical setting powder is loose, not pressed in a solid cake. Follow the directions for setting your foundation with powder, explained in Chapter 3.

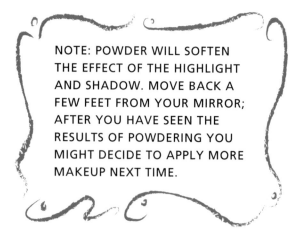

NOTE: POWDER WILL SOFTEN THE EFFECT OF THE HIGHLIGHT AND SHADOW. MOVE BACK A FEW FEET FROM YOUR MIRROR; AFTER YOU HAVE SEEN THE RESULTS OF POWDERING YOU MIGHT DECIDE TO APPLY MORE MAKEUP NEXT TIME.

Contouring Using Cosmetics

When contouring with cosmetics, only shadow is used, no highlight; therefore it is subtler. That subtlety is why it is appropriate for use offstage as well as onstage. Some cosmetics manufacturers sell pressed powder specifically for contouring; many sell bronzing powder. Either can be used as long as it coordinates with, and is darker than, your skin tone.

Using a large, rounded brush, pick up the shadow color. Follow the depression under your cheekbone, sweeping the brush from just in front of your ear until just under the outer corner of your eye. You may need to repeat this until you have the right amount. Work slowly; it is easier to add shadow than to remove it.

Use the same technique to shadow your temples and under your jawline.

Powder shadow can also be used to contour the nose. You will need a smaller brush.

CONTOURING THE CHEEKBONE WITH POWDER SHADOW

CONTOURING THE TEMPLES WITH POWDER SHADOW

CONTOURING THE JAWLINE WITH POWDER SHADOW

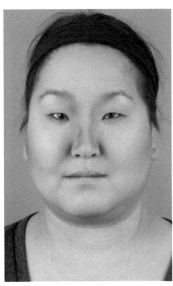

CONTOURING THE NOSE WITH POWDER SHADOW

32

For contouring the eyes, you can buy eye-shadow that comes in several shades of brown, in one of a variety of tones, all in one container. Use the lightest color for highlight and the darkest for shadow. If there is a mid-tone you can use it as a blending color; unlike cream makeup, the mixing of these colors will not become muddy. Avoid colors (such as blue, green, etc.) unless you are applying makeup for a glamor effect (which we will cover in Chapter 7) or as a character choice.

Apply powder eye-shadow similarly to cream eye-shadow.

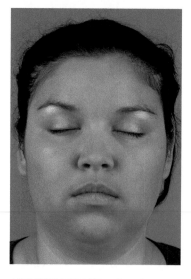

APPLYING POWDER HIGHLIGHT

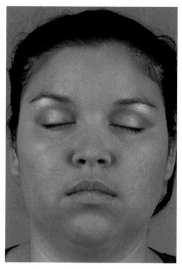

APPLYING POWDER SHADOW

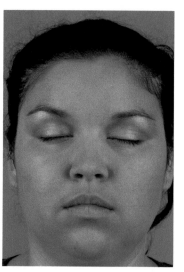

BLENDING WITH A MID-TONE

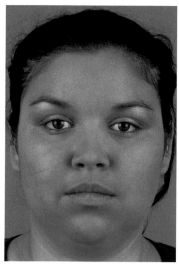

EYES CONTOURED WITH POWDER SHADOW

If the skin on your brow bone and eyelid are light enough, you may not need to use highlight. Apply bronzing powder in the crease of your eyelid with a smaller brush and blend out the edges.

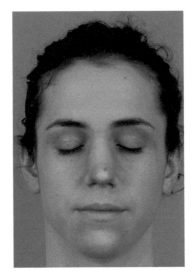 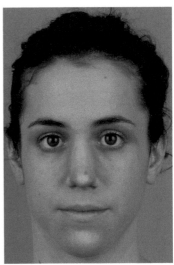

EYES CONTOURED WITH BRONZING POWDER

33

5

NATURAL BEAUTY
AND HEALTH

In Chapter 4, highlight and shadow were used to restore dimensionality to the face, focusing primarily on the bone structure. In this chapter we will look at other techniques that help define the face as well as give it natural, healthy color. The goal is to look like you are not wearing makeup.

The combination of contouring with natural health and beauty is often referred to as corrective makeup. Often, an actor will be asked to apply corrective makeup to look their healthy best and their own age.

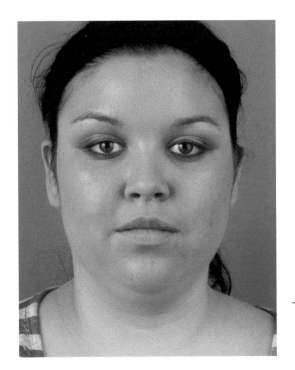

WOMAN'S UPPER AND LOWER EYELIDS LINED WITH PENCIL

Defining the Eyes

The eyes, along with the mouth, are the most expressive features of the face. Every actor wants his or her eyes to be more visible. Lining the eyes helps bring them to prominence. You can line the eyes with a well-sharpened liner pencil or a liquid liner. When you are applying makeup for a natural look, avoid a liner that is too dark for you. Unless your skin and/or hair are very dark, stick to brown liner and avoid black, otherwise it will look like you are wearing makeup.

Many women can line the top and bottom lids and still look natural. Often, when a man lines his upper lid he looks more feminine than he wants. Therefore, lining just the lower lid is a good alternative. Work towards the thinnest line you can draw. Thick eyeliner will "close up" the eye, and make the lids look smaller, which is the opposite of what is wanted.

MAN'S LOWER EYELIDS LINED WITH PENCIL

Eyeliner can also be used to give a visual lift to the outer corners of the eye if they have drooped due to age. Begin drawing the line at the inner corner of the eye. After you have reached the middle of the eye, continue drawing your line upward and away from the natural eye line.

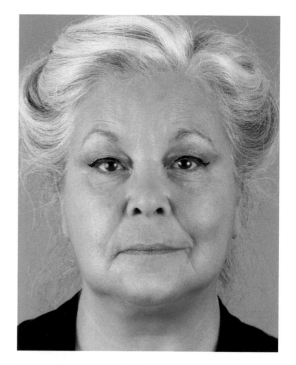

EYELINER USED TO "LIFT" THE EYE

If you are a woman with very small upper eyelids or an Asian epicanthic fold, you need to be especially careful to make the line as thin as possible. Liquid liner can help you get a very thin line. You may also try lining just the lower lid.

Women can apply mascara to accentuate their lashes. Men should use mascara only when they are playing women or if they are performing in a very large venue, because up close it can create a feminine look.

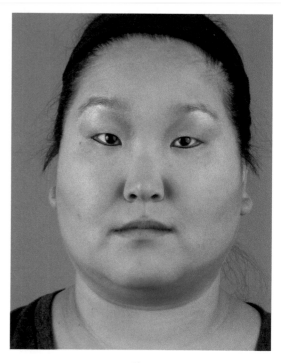

ASIAN WOMAN'S LOWER LID LINED WITH LIQUID LINER

If your eyebrows are light, or have some areas that are lighter than others, you may need to darken them. If you use an eyeliner pencil, make sure to sharpen it very well and use the side, not the point, to darken the hairs of the eyebrow. Try to avoid drawing directly on your skin, as it rarely looks natural.

Another option for darkening your eyebrows is mascara. Wipe off as much mascara from the wand as possible and carefully brush the remaining color onto the hairs of the eyebrow. Try to avoid getting it on your skin.

For a natural look a medium tone eye-shadow powder may be used to fill in sparse eyebrows. First brush with the hair, then against the hair, then with the hair a third time.

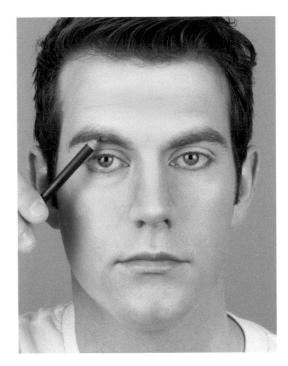

USING AN EYELINER PENCIL ON EYEBROWS

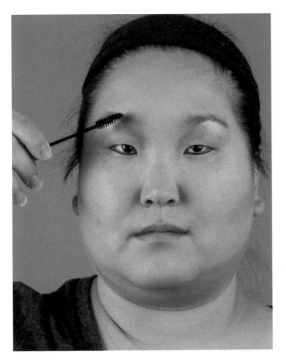

USING MASCARA ON EYEBROWS

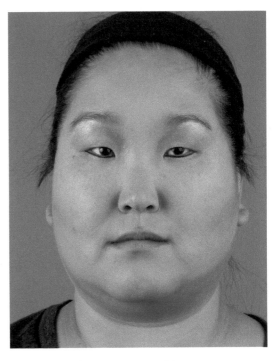

EYEBROWS DARKENED WITH MASCARA

Cheek Color

A healthy face, even a man's, will have some color on the cheeks. For a natural look, one that does not appear made-up, apply the blush in a horizontal manner across the cheekbones.

If you are using cream blush, apply it *before* you set your makeup with powder. Pick up a little of the makeup with the pad of your middle finger. Lightly tap the makeup onto your cheekbone moving left and right. Use this tapping motion to help you blend out the edges. Tapping, rather than brushing or wiping, will prevent you from obliterating your highlight and shadow contouring.

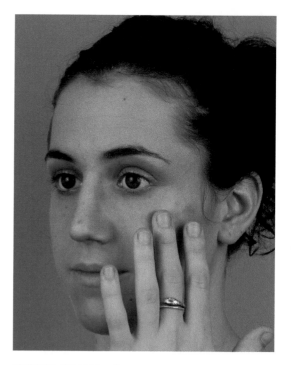

TAPPING CREAM BLUSH ONTO CHEEKBONE

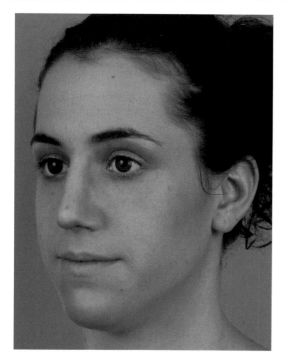

CREAM BLUSH ON WOMAN

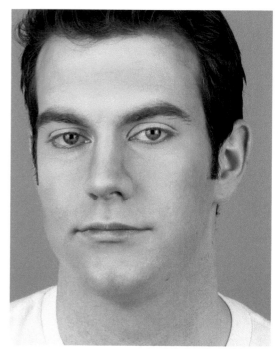

CREAM BLUSH ON MAN

If you are using powder blush, apply it *after* you set your makeup with powder. Pick up a little of the makeup with a large, rounded brush and lightly brush it back and forth across your cheekbone. Blend out the edges for a natural look.

Blush can also be used judiciously across the forehead, on the nose and on the chin for an all-over rosy glow.

APPLYING POWDER BLUSH

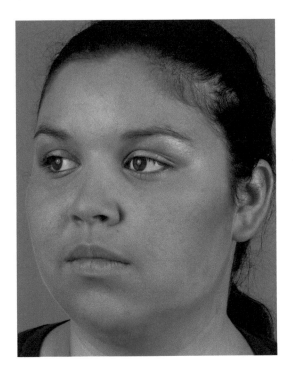

BLENDED POWDER BLUSH

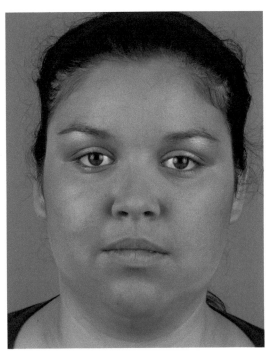

BLUSH APPLIED ALL OVER FOR A HEALTHY GLOW

Defining the Lips

Apply lip color *before* you use setting powder. Women should use a lip-lining pencil to follow the outline of the lips. Use your medium or small flat brush to blend the inside of the pencil line inwards, leaving the outer edge sharp.

Use your medium or small flat brush to pick up a small amount of neutral cream lip color and fill in the outline.

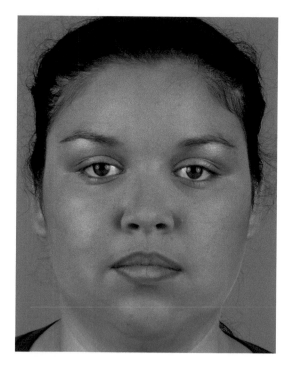

LINING THE LIPS

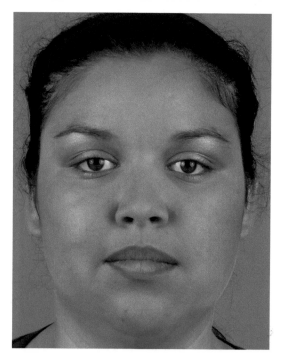

BLENDING THE LIP LINE INWARDS

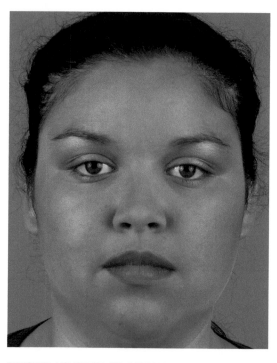

FINISHED LIP COLOR ON A WOMAN

Men can apply neutral cream lip color and follow the shape of their lips without using the liner pencil. If the most neutral lip color available seems too feminine, mix some base into it to bring it closer to your skin tone.

If this is your final step, set your makeup with powder.

FINISHED LIP COLOR ON A MAN

6

MANIPULATING
THE BONE STRUCTURE

Highlight and shadow are used to manipulate the bone structure of your face for a number of reasons. Many people feel that they have slight imperfections, such as crooked nose or a receding chin, and want to make corrections. An actor may be playing a character that is described in the play as having a specific type of feature or look that she needs to replicate. A performer may want to accentuate or deemphasize features to support the type of character he is playing, perhaps a larger forehead for a pedantic professor, or a strong, square jawline for a classical Greek hero.

In this chapter, the same highlight and shadow techniques used in Chapter 4 will be used to change the appearance of the shape of your features.

Manipulating the Forehead

In Chapter 4 highlight was applied to the ridges of the forehead. The highlight extended horizontally just until the edge of the temples. To widen the forehead, extend the highlight on the ridges out onto the temples.

Apply the shadow in between the ridges at the same length as the highlight. Apply the shadow on the temples, beginning further out than you normally would.

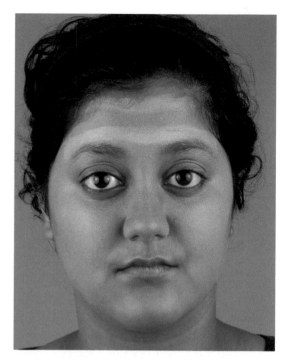

EXTENDED HIGHLIGHT ON RIDGES OF FOREHEAD

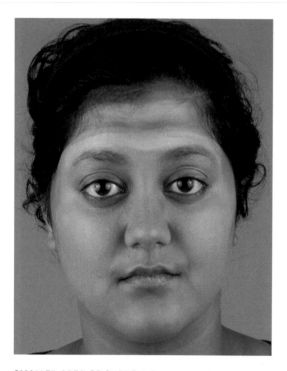

SMALLER AREA OF SHADOW ON TEMPLES

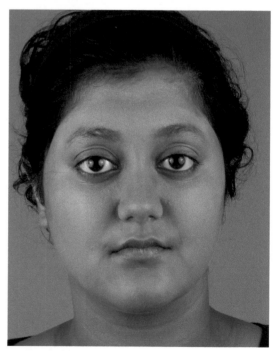

BLENDED HIGHLIGHT AND SHADOW TO WIDEN FOREHEAD

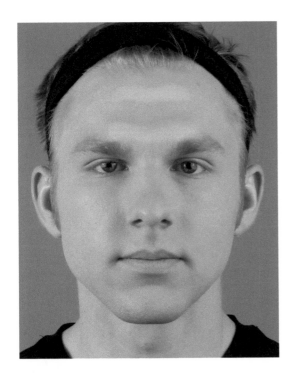

HIGHLIGHT TO NARROW FOREHEAD

To narrow the forehead, apply shorter swaths of highlight to the ridges and a shorter swath of shadow to the depression in between. Apply shadows to the temples closer in on the forehead.

NOTE: NARROWING YOUR FEATURES WILL MAKE YOUR FACE LOOK LONGER. WIDENING YOUR FEATURES WILL MAKE YOUR FACE LOOK SHORTER.

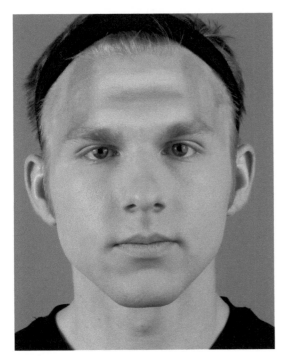

SHADOW TO NARROW FOREHEAD

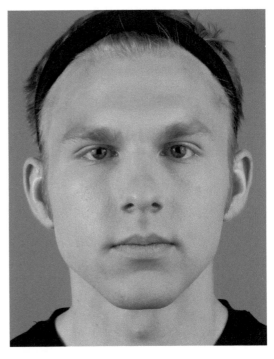

BLENDED HIGHLIGHT AND SHADOW ON NARROWED FOREHEAD

To make the forehead appear shorter or lower, apply swaths of highlight slightly below the upper ridge.

Apply shadow in between the ridges and on the temples as for normal contouring. Apply shadow above the top ridge, just below the hairline.

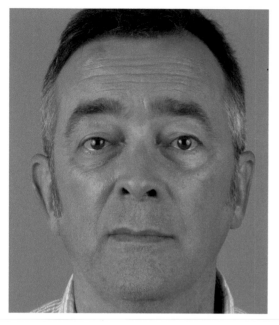

BEFORE CONTOURING. Model, Nick Newman

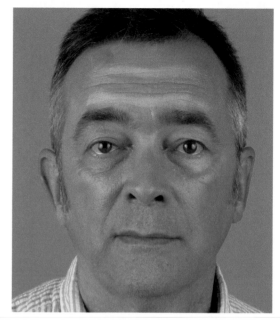

HIGHLIGHT TO SHORTEN FOREHEAD

SHADOW TO SHORTEN FOREHEAD

BLENDED HIGHLIGHT AND SHADOW

46

Manipulating the Cheekbones

Making your cheekbones appear higher will give your face a narrower or sunken in look. Instead of applying the highlight to the vertical, outward-facing plane of the cheekbones, apply the highlight slightly above that, partially on top of the cheekbone. Be careful not to intrude into the eye socket.

Apply the shadow a little higher than you normally would.

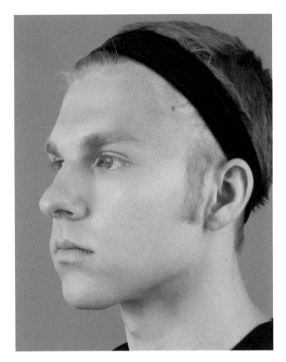

HIGHLIGHT ON TOP OF CHEEKBONE

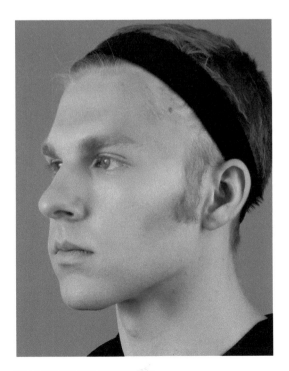

SHADOW BELOW CHEEKBONE

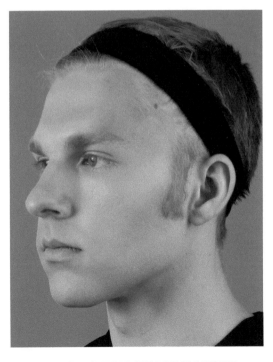

BLENDED HIGHLIGHT AND SHADOW FOR HIGHER CHEEKBONE

If your face is wide, and you want to make it look narrower, you can shorten your cheekbones by leaving space between the beginning of your highlight and the front of your ear.

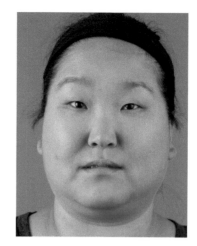

HIGHLIGHT STARTED FURTHER IN ON CHEEKBONE

You can apply shadow just in front of your ear to make the end of the cheekbone recede. Apply shadow under the cheekbone.

SHADOW FOR NARROW FACE   **BLENDED HIGHLIGHT AND SHADOW FOR NARROW FACE**

Manipulating the Nose

To make your nose appear longer and thinner, use your thin flat brush. Apply highlight down the center of the nose beginning on the lower ridge of your forehead and extending beyond the tip of your nose.

Apply a swath of shadow on either side of the bridge of the nose, extending down over the nares and to the tip. Leave room to blend. There will be less room in between the highlight and shadow than for normal contouring. Blend.

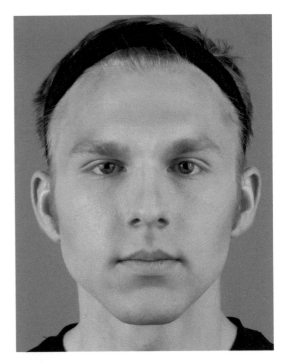

HIGHLIGHT FOR LONG, THIN NOSE

49

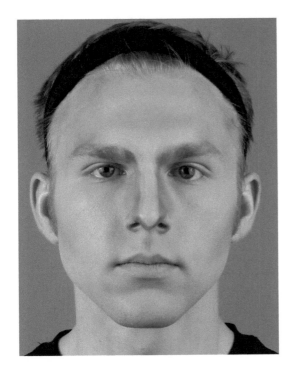

SHADOW FOR A LONG, THIN NOSE

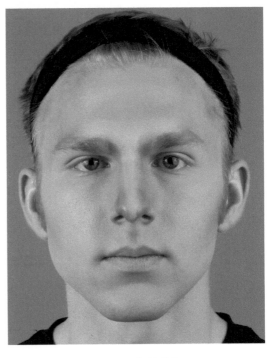

BLENDED HIGHLIGHT AND SHADOW

To make the nose appear shorter and wider, use the flat side of your wide flat brush. Apply highlight down the center of the nose beginning on the bridge and stopping before you get to the tip.

Apply a swath of shadow on either side of the bridge of the nose, ending at and surrounding the nares, leaving some room to blend. Apply a short swath of shadow just above the bridge of the nose and under the tip of the nose. Blend.

Shadowing under the tip of the nose will also make it appear shorter.

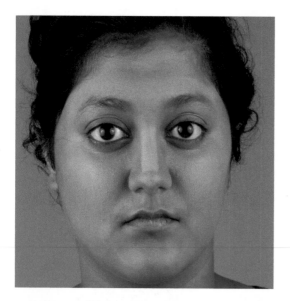

HIGHLIGHT FOR SHORT, WIDE NOSE

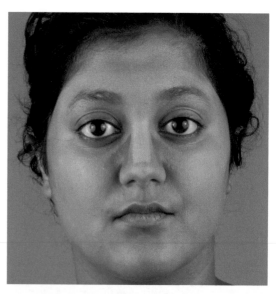

SHADOW FOR A SHORT, WIDE NOSE

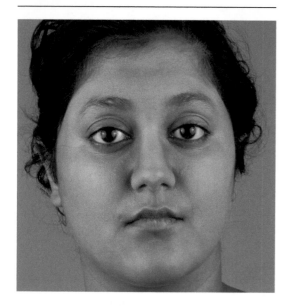

BLENDED HIGHLIGHT AND SHADOW

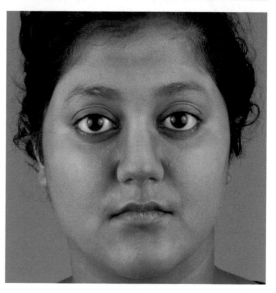

SHADOW UNDER TIP OF NOSE.

To make the nose appear upturned, use your medium flat brush. Apply highlight down the center of the nose beginning on the bridge and stopping before the ball of the nose. Apply a dot of highlight above the center of the ball of the nose.

Shadow the sides as normal. Apply a short swath of shadow just above the bridge of the nose. Apply an arc of shadow under the tip of the nose. Shadow in between the bottom of the center highlight on the bridge, and the dot of highlight on the ball of the nose. Blend.

51

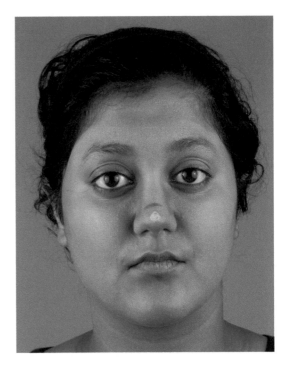

HIGHLIGHT AND SHADOW FOR UPTURNED NOSE

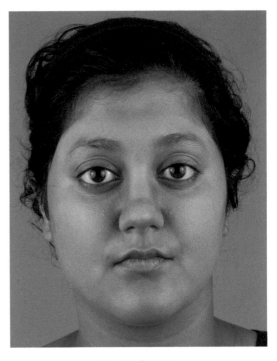

BLENDED HIGHLIGHT AND SHADOW

To make the nose appear broken, apply the highlight in a crooked shape. Frame the crooked highlight shape with shadow. Blend.

52

HIGHLIGHT FOR BROKEN NOSE

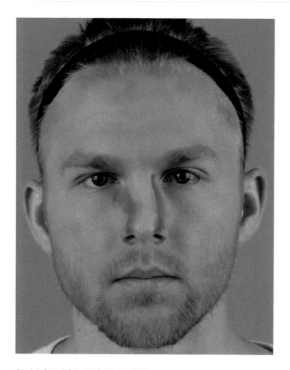

SHADOW FOR BROKEN NOSE

BLENDED HIGHLIGHT AND SHADOW

Manipulating the Jawline

You can make a square jawline curved or a curved jawline square by applying highlight in the shape you want and framing it with shadow underneath. Make sure you leave some room to blend out your edges.

CURVING A SQUARE JAWLINE. Model, Emilio Sotelo

BLENDED HIGHLIGHT AND SHADOW

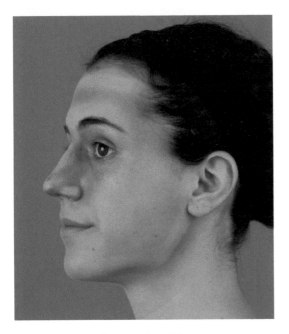

SQUARING OFF A CURVED JAWLINE

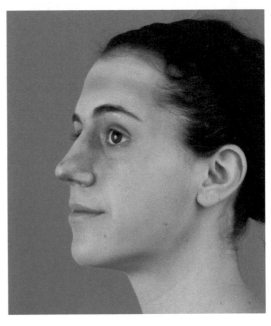

BLENDED HIGHLIGHT AND SHADOW

You can make the face appear narrower by beginning the highlight on the jawline further in on the face.

Apply the shadow right behind it, in front of the bottom of the ear. Shadowing down onto the neck will help it recede and the jawline stand out.

HIGHLIGHT ON JAWLINE TO NARROW FACE

SHADOW ON JAWLINE AND NECK TO NARROW FACE

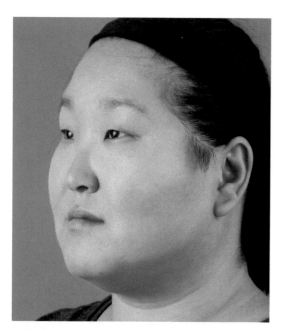

BLENDED HIGHLIGHT AND SHADOW

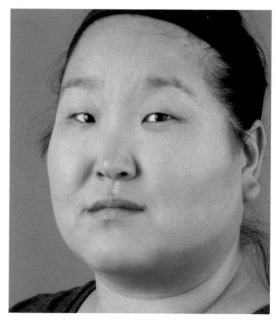

For those who have reached the age where the jawline had begun to sag, careful contouring can bring back a bit of youth. Apply the highlight with a slight, upward curve.

Apply shadow following the same curve. Blend.

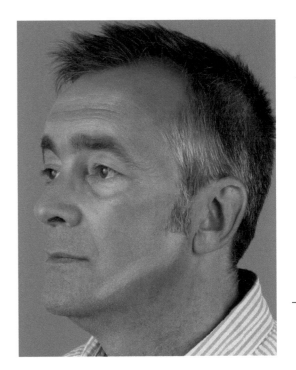

HIGHLIGHT TO RAISE THE JAWLINE

55

SHADOW TO RAISE THE JAWLINE

BLENDED HIGHLIGHT AND SHADOW

A similar technique can be used with bronzing powder or powder shadow in a very small theatre space or even for everyday wear.

JAWLINE BEFORE SHADOW

POWDER SHADOW TO RAISE JAWLINE

POWDER SHADOW BLENDED

Manipulating the Chin

You can make the chin look rounder by putting a dot of highlight just above the middle and blending it out in a spiral manner. Apply an arc of shadow around the bottom of the chin. Blend.

You can make the large chin look smaller by moving the shadow up higher, closer to the dot of highlight.

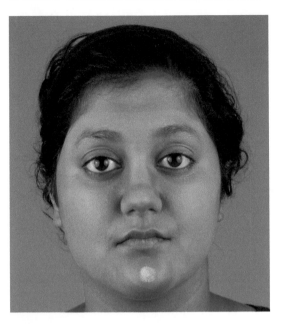

HIGHLIGHT AND SHADOW FOR ROUNDED CHIN

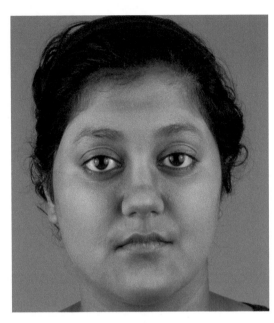

BLENDED HIGHLIGHT AND SHADOW

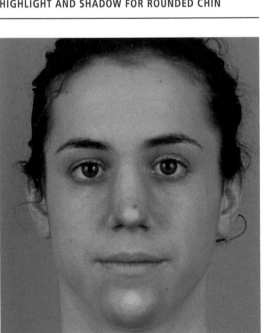

HIGHLIGHT AND SHADOW FOR SMALLER CHIN

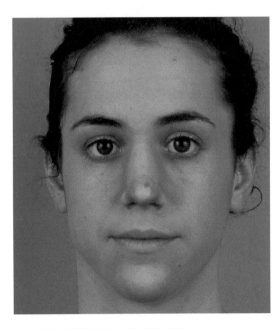

BLENDED HIGHLIGHT AND SHADOW

You can make the small chin look larger by moving the shadow lower and wider.

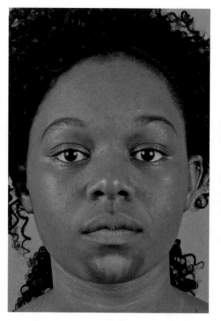 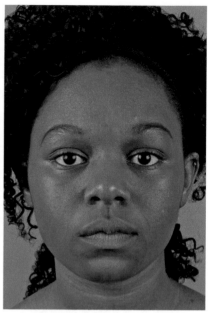

HIGHLIGHT AND SHADOW FOR LARGER CHIN. Model, Ryan Woods

BLENDED HIGHLIGHT AND SHADOW

You can make the chin look long and pointy by applying a line of highlight and a "V" of shadow.

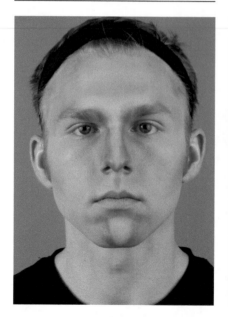 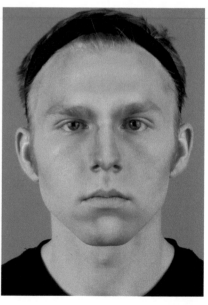

HIGHLIGHT AND SHADOW FOR POINTY CHIN

BLENDED HIGHLIGHT AND SHADOW

58

NOTE: IF THIS IS YOUR FINAL STEP, SET THE MAKEUP WITH POWDER.

7

GLAMOUR

There are many contemporary books and magazines can instruct you in the application of street makeup for contemporary female glamour. Fashions in street makeup are continually changing. This chapter will cover a few basic techniques using both theatrical makeup and street makeup for a classic, timeless twenty-first-century glamour. The following techniques should be used *after* you have powdered your base.

Emphasizing the Eyes

The western standard of beauty for women has, for many years, included large, deep-set eyes with a prominent brow-bone. The technique for achieving this look was demonstrated in Chapter 5. When applying makeup for glamour, and when you are not trying to hide the fact that you are wearing makeup, you can use colors that do not match your skin tone (blues, greens, etc.) and colors that have shimmer or metallic in them. However, the same basic concepts of highlight and shadow apply; use lighter colors to make features stand out and darker colors to make features recede.

Choose two or three shades of the same color in a dry, powder eye-shadow. They can be bought separately, or you can buy three or four coordinating tones grouped in one package.

Apply the lightest color to the outer half of the brow-bone directly under the brow, and on the center of the eyelid.

Apply the darkest color to the crease above the lid.

Use the mid-tone to blend the light and dark shades. Unlike cream makeup, powder eye-shadows will not turn muddy when blended together, if they are similar in tone.

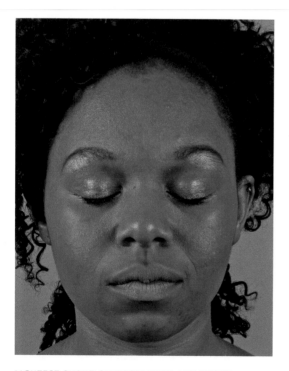

LIGHTEST SHADE ON BROW BONE AND EYELID

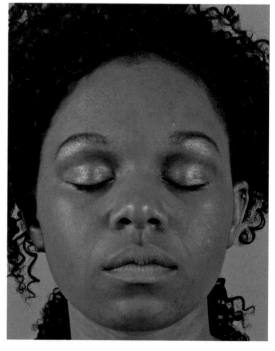

DARKEST SHADE IN CREASE

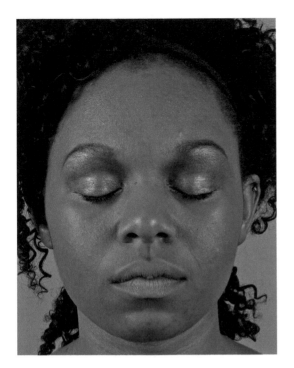
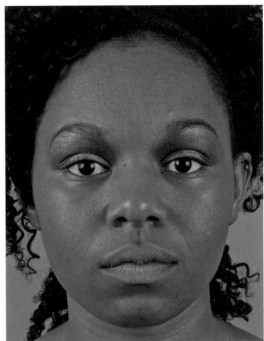

THREE SHADES BLENDED

The western standard of beauty for women also dictates that the eyes should be as far apart as they are wide. Eyeliner is often used to make the eyes look wider apart than they actually are. Instead of beginning the eyeliner at the very inner corner of the eye, leave a space before beginning. You can also widen the liner as it reaches the outer corner of the eye. The liner on the lower lid can begin as far out as the center of the eye.

Before darkening the eyebrows, make certain that they are cleanly tweezed. The eyebrows should be brushed up and out so the hairs follow the natural arch. Follow instructions for darkening eyebrows in Chapter 5.

Mascara should be used on upper and lower lashes. If your lashes are thin, false eyelashes are available. Instructions are usually included in the packaging. As with any new products, test the adhesive to make certain that you do not have an allergic reaction.

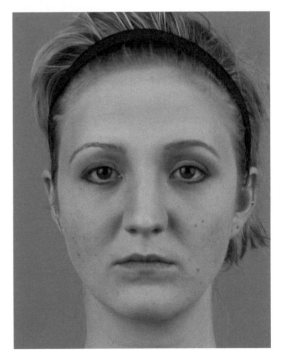

LINER ON UPPER LID TO WIDEN EYES. Model, Devin Tumpkin

Emphasizing Asian Eyes

Asian eyes, specifically the lids, have become quite politicized. In order to "be more marketable" a number of actors and media personalities of Asian heritage have had plastic surgery to make their eyes appear more western. The following technique will not redesign, or westernize, but rather emphasize the beauty of, the natural female Asian eye.

Apply the lightest shade of eye-shadow to the entire upper lid and to the brow bone under the outer eyebrow. Apply a small amount of the darkest shade of eye-shadow to the inner corner of the epicanthic fold near the nose. Apply the middle tone of eye-shadow to the rest of the fold and use it to blend the edges of the lighter and darker eye-shadow colors.

Use eyeliner on lower lid and extend beyond outer corner of eye. Apply mascara. Follow instructions for eyebrows in Chapter 5.

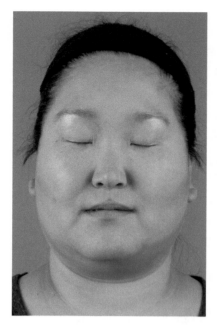

LIGHTEST EYE-SHADOW ON LID AND BROW BONE

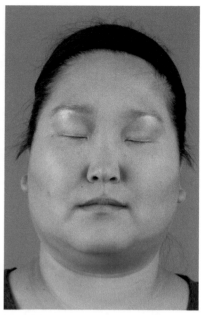

DARKEST EYE-SHADOW COLOR ON INNER CORNER

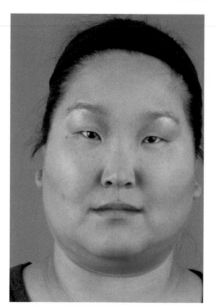

MIDDLE TONE ON FOLD; THREE COLORS OF SHADOW BLENDED

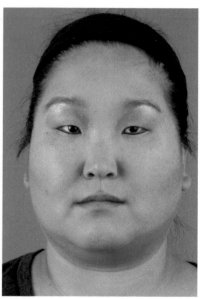

COMPLETED EYE MAKEUP

Emphasizing the Cheeks

For a natural look blush is applied horizontally. For glamour it can be applied at an angle.

Emphasizing the Mouth

Full, rounded lips are generally the norm for glamour. If your lips are already full, follow their natural shape with lip-liner and fill then in with cream color, as demonstrated in Chapter 5. Lips can be made to appear fuller by extending their outline using a lip-liner pencil. Because you are not trying to hide the fact that you are wearing makeup, you may choose a color much different than your natural lip color. However, make certain that the lip-liner is only slightly darker than the lip color; lip outlines are never glamorous.

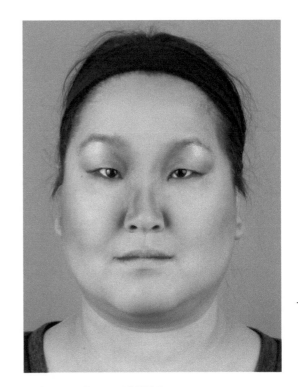

ANGLED BLUSH APPLICATION

63

LINER USED TO MAKE LIPS APPEAR FULLER

FINISHED LIP COLOR

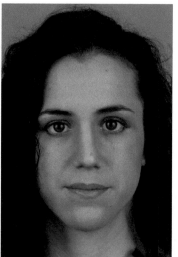
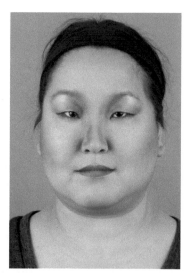

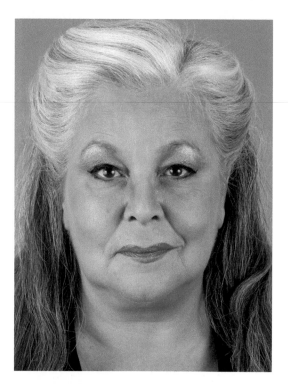
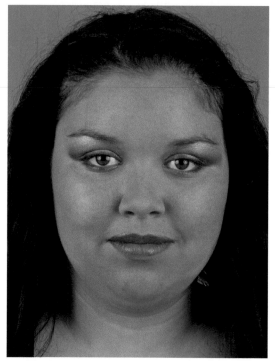

MAKEUP FOR GLAMOUR

8

MANIPULATING CARTILAGE, MUSCLE, AND FAT

A performer may be called on to play a character that is heavier than he or she is, or has personal traits that might suggest roundness in their features. This chapter will demonstrate the way highlight and shadow can help create the appearance of roundness in facial features or, in the case of the lips, make them appear thinner. Note that those with very angular faces and little subcutaneous fat may have trouble with some of the features in this chapter. Of consolation is the fact that it will be easier to make your face appear exceedingly thin.

66

Rounded "Apple" Cheeks

To find the proper placement of highlight and shadow for rounded "apple" cheeks, one must smile hard. Not a grin, but a full smile that reveals the teeth. If there is any subcutaneous fat on your face, your big smile will create a rounded shape on the cheek, directly below the eye socket.

Using the pad of your middle finger, apply a dot of highlight to your cheek just above the center of the rounded shape. Relax the face. You may need to try this several times to find the right location.

Smile again. Apply an arc of shadow below the center of the rounded "apple" cheek. Notice the amount of distance left for blending between the highlight and the shadow.

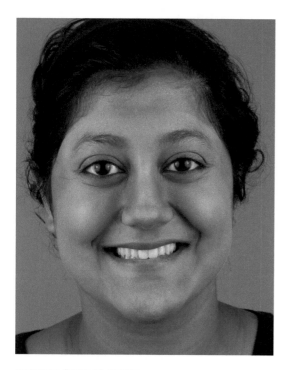

NATURAL "APPLE" CHEEK

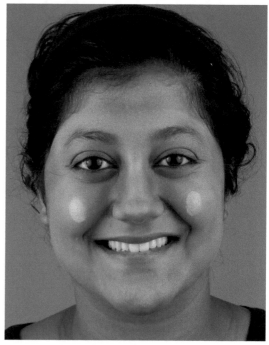

HIGHLIGHT ON "APPLE" CHEEK

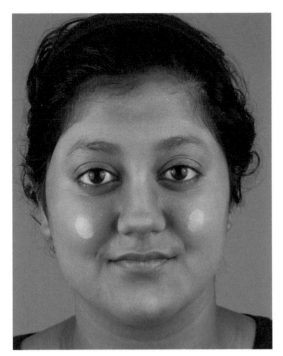

HIGHLIGHT ON RELAXED CHEEK

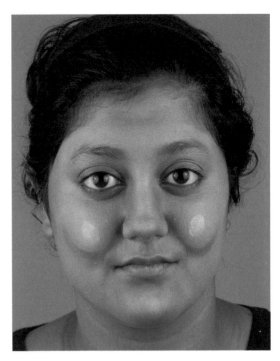

SHADOW ON "APPLE" CHEEK

Blend the highlight in a spiral manner. The finger is the best tool for blending in a circle or spiral. Blend the shadows' upper and lower edges following the curve of the arc.

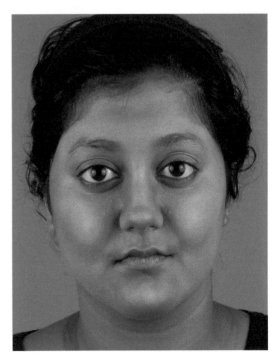

BLENDED HIGHLIGHT AND SHADOW

A similar method can be used to make an actor look younger. Age will cause the cheekbones to become more prominent due to the deterioration of subcutaneous fat. A plumper, rounder cheek can give the impression of youth.

Apply the highlight a little higher than you would for an apple cheek which is used to give the impression of heaviness. Apply the arc of shadow slightly higher as well, so it does not touch the nasolabial fold.

HIGHLIGHT FOR YOUTHFUL "APPLE" CHEEK

SHADOW FOR YOUTHFUL "APPLE" CHEEK

BLENDED HIGHLIGHT AND SHADOW

Rounded and Widened Nose

To accentuate or exaggerate the roundness of the nose, treat the ball of the nose in the same way as the "apple" cheek. Apply a dot of highlight just above the center. Apply an arc of shadow below the center of the ball of the nose.

Blend carefully—this is a small area.

In Chapter 6, highlight and shadow were used on the bridge of the nose to widen and shorten it. Use this technique to support the roundness of the ball of the nose.

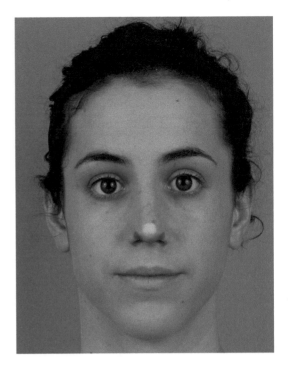

HIGHLIGHT AND SHADOW ON BALL OF NOSE

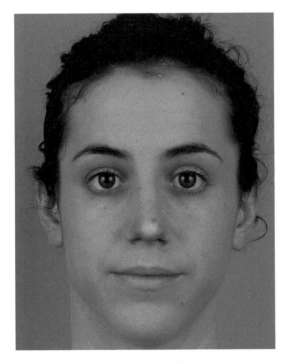

BLENDED HIGHLIGHT AND SHADOW

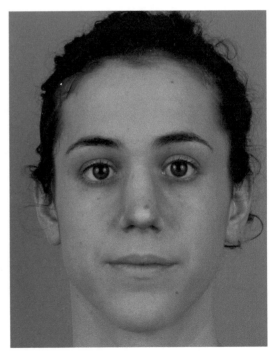

WIDENED BRIDGE WITH ROUNDED TIP

Double Chins

If you apply highlight and shadow to your neck you must first apply foundation as far down as you plan to extend the contouring. Take into consideration the height or depth of the neckline of your costume. Next, apply highlight and shadow for a rounded chin as demonstrated in Chapter 4. Now tilt your chin down and pull it back in towards your neck. This will create rolls of skin on which you can simulate fat.

Use your wide brush to apply highlight to the outermost parts of the skin rolls, tapering out the width at the ends.

Release the neck; a faint trace of the creases will remain. Apply shadow in the creases between the rolls, creating a hard edge at the bottom and a softer, blended edge above.

Blend carefully, leaving base tone in-between.

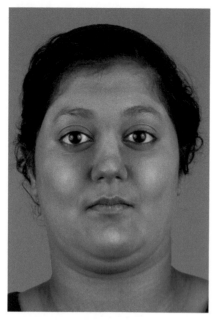

CREATING ROLLS OF SKIN

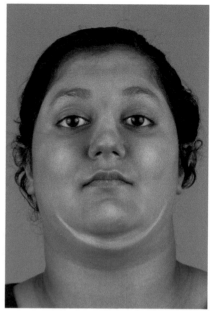

HIGHLIGHT OUTER PART OF ROLLS

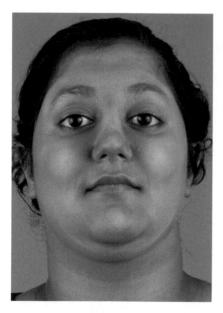

SHADOW IN THE CREASES

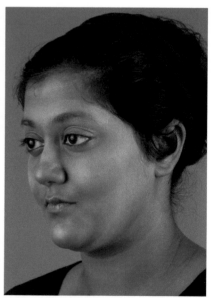

BLENDED HIGHLIGHT AND SHADOW

Changing the Shape of the Lips

Depending on the character you are playing or the time period of the play, there a several changes you may want to make to the shape of your lips. To make your lips appear fuller, draw the shape you want with your lip-liner pencil. Use your medium or small flat brush to blend the inside of the pencil line inwards, leaving the outer edge sharp.

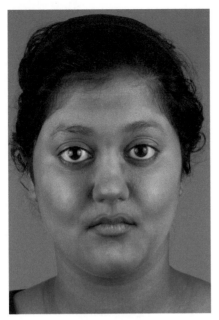

CREATING A FULLER LIP WITH LIP-LINER

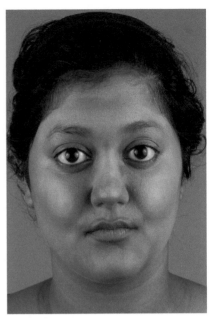

FILLED IN LIPS

Use your medium or small flat brush to fill in the outline with cream lip color.

If there is not enough contrast between the tone of the lips and the foundation, carefully outline the lips with cream highlight makeup.

Blend the highlight out and away from the lips.

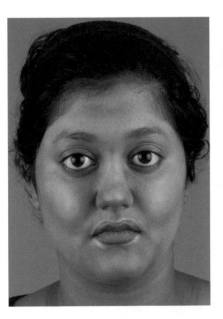

LINING THE LIPS WITH HIGHLIGHT

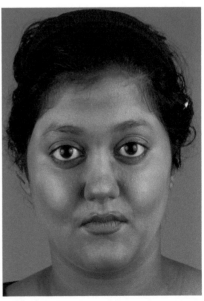

HIGHLIGHT HELPS THE LIPS STAND OUT FROM THE FOUNDATION

To make your lips appear thinner, draw the shape you want with your lip-liner pencil.

Blend the inside of the pencil line inwards, leaving the outer edge sharp.

Use your medium or small flat brush to fill in the outline with cream lip color.

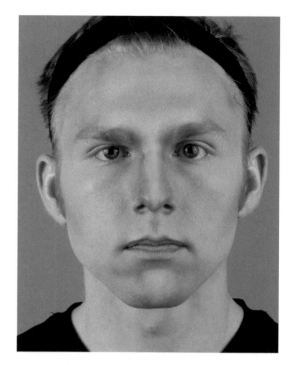

CREATING A THINNER LIP LINE WITH LIP PENCIL

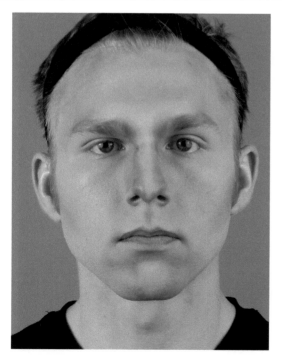

BLENDED LIP PENCIL LINE

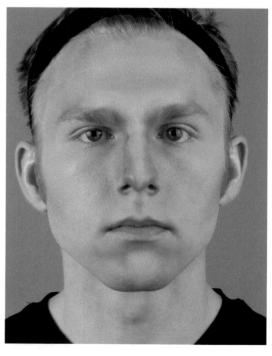

FILLED IN LIP LINE

To block out the natural color of your own lips, use your small flat brush to follow the shape of your new lip line with cream highlight. Keep the inner edge of your highlight sharp and blend the outer edge.

Apply cream foundation over the highlight in the same manner

If this is your final step, set your makeup with powder.

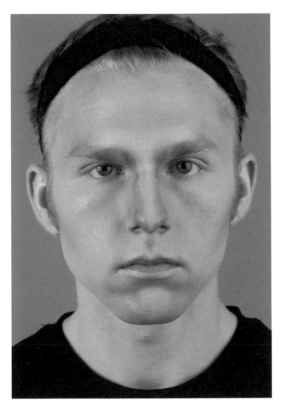

HIGHLIGHTING TO BLOCK OUT LIPS

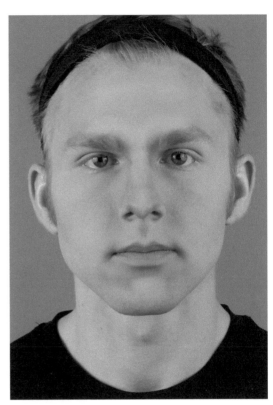

THINNER LIPS

9

AGING

Many people think that they know, intuitively, what age looks like on the face. But it is very important to do visual research before applying age makeup, otherwise you might end up indicating the look of age rather than replicating it. If you resemble any biological relatives who are older than you, they can be a wealth of research. I look a lot like my mother, so, were I to age my face, it would be helpful for me to study the particular way her face has aged. Or I could look at photographs of my grandmother, who I also resemble. Take as many pictures of your subject as possible and use them for reference as you are applying your makeup. If you have no contact with your biological relatives, find pictures of people with your particular ethnic background to use as a resource.

When aging the face with makeup, it is helpful to think about gravity. The longer you are alive, the more time gravity has to pull down on your face. Also remember that as we age, the skin loses elasticity and some of its subcutaneous fat. Therefore, much of what you do to age your face with makeup involves creating the impression that the skin has responded to these forces by dropping.

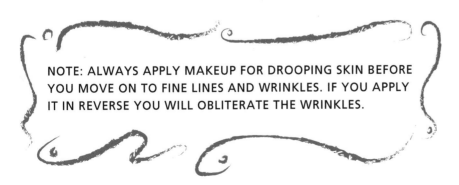

NOTE: ALWAYS APPLY MAKEUP FOR DROOPING SKIN BEFORE YOU MOVE ON TO FINE LINES AND WRINKLES. IF YOU APPLY IT IN REVERSE YOU WILL OBLITERATE THE WRINKLES.

Eye Bags

One of the first places the face starts to show its age is in the delicate tissue underneath the eyes. There is no muscle or fat in this area, therefore there is nothing to hold the skin up and out.

If you naturally have dark circles under your eyes, or have very deep-set eyes, you may be able to see where to place your eye bags. If not, you may have to gently pull down on the skin to see where it would drop or press up on your cheeks to find the crease of the eye socket.

Use your wide flat brush to apply a swath of highlight below the eye socket, above the cheek, following the curve. Keep the upper edge next to the socket sharp; allow the lower edge to fade out.

Blend the lower edge. This highlight will help to accentuate the shadow above it. You may already be able to see the shadow of the eye socket more clearly.

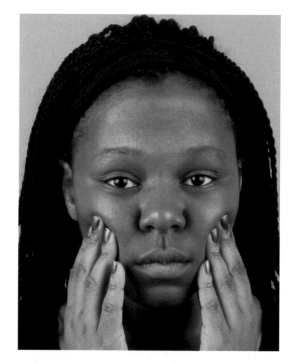

FINDING PLACEMENT FOR EYE BAGS

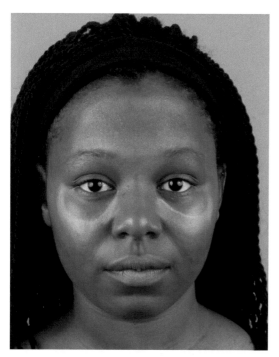

HIGHLIGHT BELOW EYE BAG

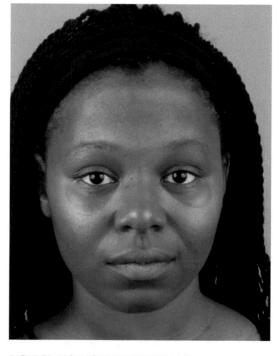

BLENDED HIGHLIGHT BELOW EYE BAG

Use your small flat brush to apply an arc of highlight between the lower eyelid and the bottom edge of the eye socket.

Blend the upper and lower edges.

Use your small brush to apply an arc of shadow at the bottom of the eye socket, right up against the lower highlight, following the curve. *It is very important that you do not get any shadow onto the highlight below it.* Keep the lower edge sharp; allow the upper edge to fade out.

Blend the upper edge.

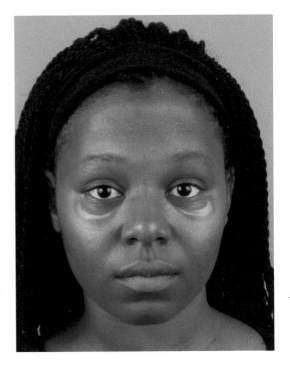

HIGHLIGHTING THE EYE BAG

BLENDED HIGHLIGHT OF EYE BAG

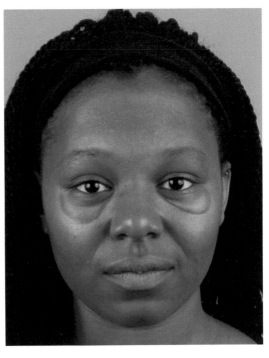

SHADOWING THE EYE BAG

78

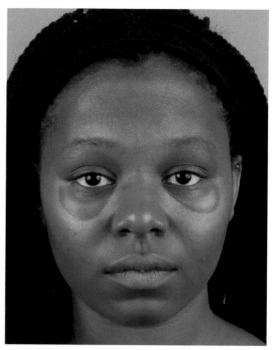

BLENDED SHADOW OF EYE BAG

You can create smaller eye bags by focusing on the area close to the nose and stopping by the middle of the eye. This can be done for the less extensive aging needed to create the appearance of middle age.

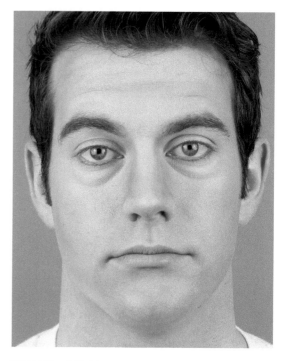

SMALLER, LESS AGED EYE BAGS

Droopy Eyelids and Eyebrows

The section of the eyelid directly below the eyebrow is known as the orbital part of the eyelid. This is another area of the face that begins to fall in the earlier stages of aging. You will notice a diagonal drop, with the lower end falling at the outside corners of the eye. To find the placement of your droopy eyelid, or orbital part, gently press down on the outer end of your eyebrow to create a crease near the corner of your eye.

Use your medium flat brush to apply a swath of highlight below the crease you have created, following the curve. Keep the upper edge next to the crease sharp; allow the lower edge to fade out. Blend the lower edge.

Use your small flat brush to apply a curved, diagonal swath, or "swoosh," of highlight on the orbital part between the outer eyebrow and crease you have created.

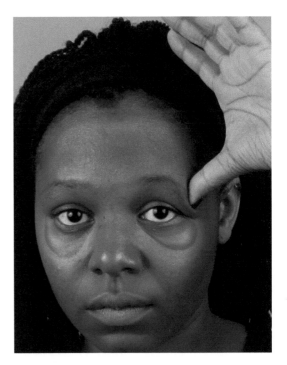

FINDING PLACEMENT FOR THE DROOPY EYELID

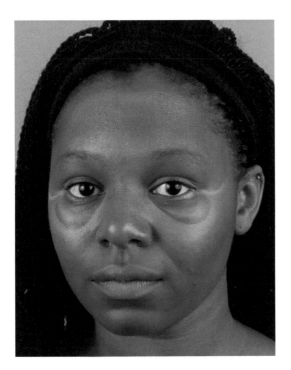

HIGHLIGHT BELOW DROOPY EYELID

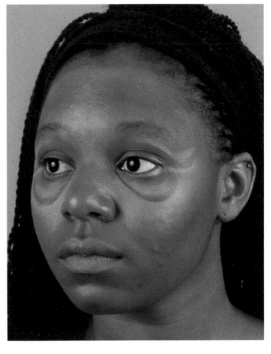

HIGHLIGHTING THE DROOPY EYELID

Blend the upper and lower edges of the highlight "swoosh.".

Use your small brush to apply a swath of shadow in the crease you have created, right up against the lower highlight, following the curve. Keep the lower edge against the crease sharp; allow the upper edge to fade out.

Blend the upper edge of the shadow.

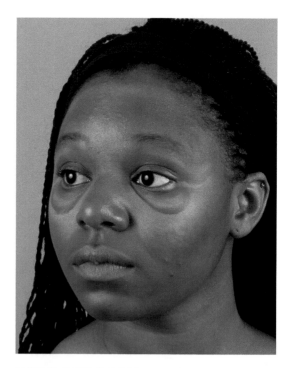

BLENDED HIGHLIGHT OF THE DROOPY EYELID

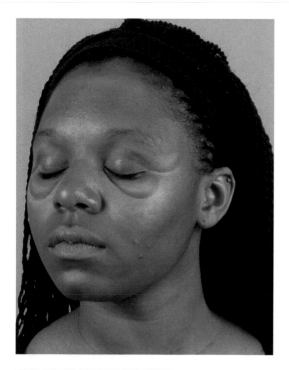

SHADOWING THE DROOPY EYELID

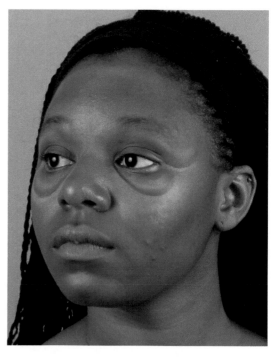

BLENDED SHADOW OF THE DROOPY EYELID

If you have room underneath your outer eyebrow, apply some shadow following the shape of the "swoosh"; this will help to visually push down the highlight on the orbital part. Brush your eyebrows down, to accentuate the direction of droopiness.

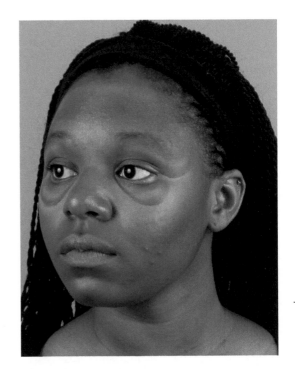

SHADOW UNDER EYEBROW

If the character you are playing is not one to use eyebrow pencil, you can brush theatrical liquid hair whitener onto the hairs of the eyebrow.

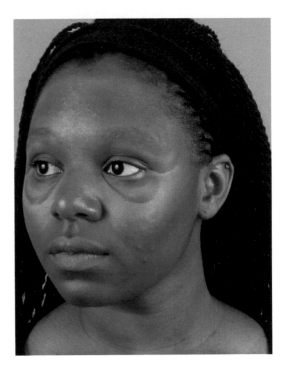

USING EYEBROWS TO ACCENTUATE DROOPY EYE LID

Longer Nose

As you age, your nose continues to grow. Unless you are creating the appearance of a rounded ball of the nose, extend the highlight on the bridge to the tip or even beyond. Continue the shadow on either side to support the highlight.

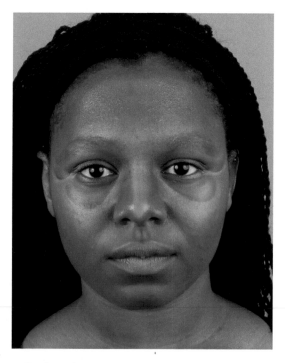

NOSE LENGTHENED AT THE TIP

BLENDED HIGHLIGHT

Nasolabial Folds

The creases that connect the upper part of the nares of the nose to the outer corners of the lips are the nasolabial folds or furrows. You can find the correct placement for these creases by smiling hard. When you relax, a trace of the creases will remain.

FINDING THE NASOLABIAL FOLDS

Use your medium flat brush to apply a swath of highlight inside the crease you have created, towards the center of the face, following the curve. Keep the edge that touches the crease sharp; allow the inner edge to fade out.

Blend the inner edge.

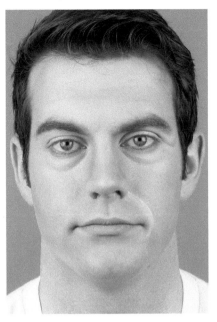 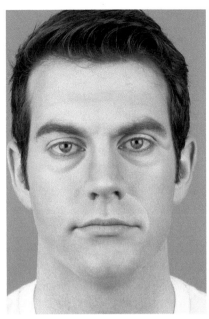

INNER HIGHLIGHT OF NASOLABIAL FOLD

BLENDED INNER EDGE OF HIGHLIGHT

Use your small flat brush to apply a swath of highlight on your cheek, parallel to the previous highlight. Leave room for the shadow.

Blend both edges of this highlight.

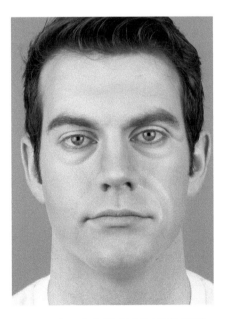 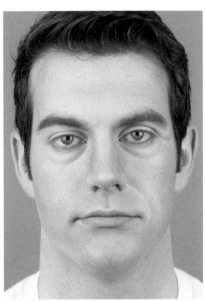

OUTER HIGHLIGHT OF NASOLABIAL FOLD

BLENDED OUTER HIGHLIGHT

Use your small brush to apply a swath of shadow in the crease, right up against the inner highlight, following the curve. Keep the inner edge against the crease sharp; allow the outer edge to fade out.

Blend the outer edge.

If you want to add weight to your character as well as age, omit the outer highlights, and create rounded "apple" cheeks as described in Chapter 8. The shadow of the cheek connects to the shadow of the nasolabial fold.

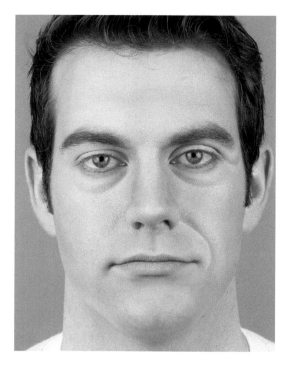

SHADOWING THE NASOLABIAL FOLDS

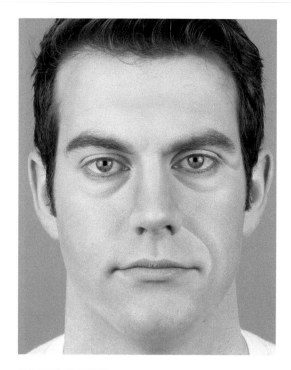

BLENDED SHADOW

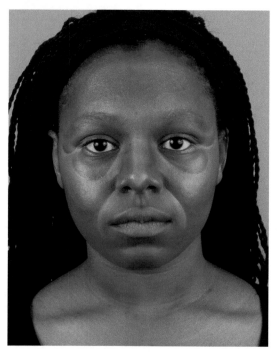

NASOLABIAL FOLDS WITH ROUNDED CHEEKS

Frown Lines

When you frown, you create vertical creases from the outer corners of the mouth that are very similar to the nasolabial folds. Apply highlights and shadows to these creases in the same way as you would the nasolabial folds.

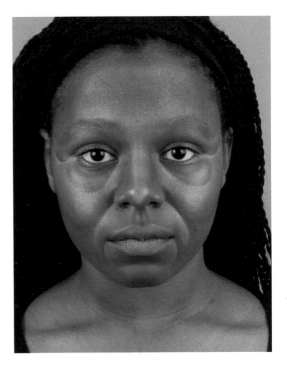

FROWN LINES

Aging the Jawline

As you age, the skin along the jawline will begin to fall into jowls. Pull your chin into your neck and gently press the skin down to see what it will look like as it droops. As with the double chin, you will see how the skin of the face connects to the skin on the neck.

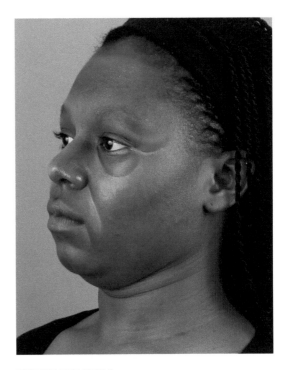

FINDING THE JOWLS

Use your wide brush to apply a swath of highlight along the jawline, starting in front of the lower ear. Continue down along the fold of skin you have created.

Use your wide brush to apply a swath of shadow under the highlight, leaving room to blend. Apply a swath of shadow in front of the highlight leaving room to blend.

Blend all edges.

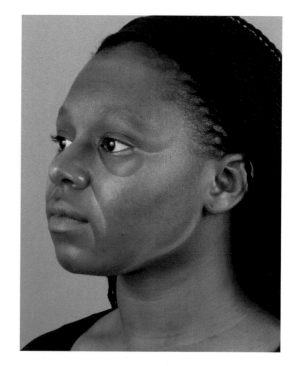

HIGHLIGHTING THE JOWLS

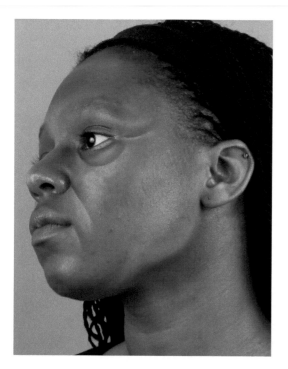

SHADOWING THE JOWLS

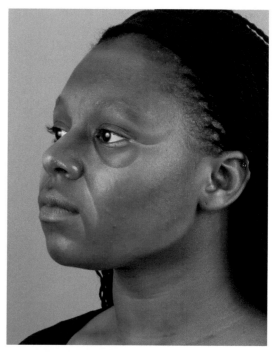

COMPLETED JOWLS

Fine Lines and Wrinkles

The previous techniques can be used to age a young actor up into their healthy forties or early fifties. By the time one has reached their sixties and seventies, or if they have lived a hard or unhealthy life, one will have developed visible wrinkles.

Fine lines and wrinkles appear on the surface of the skin, and do not involve cartilage, muscle or fat. They can be considered a surface texture. As a surface texture, wrinkles should be applied *after* all of the makeup for droopy skin has been applied rather than before. The smallest brush is used and the application is very delicate; applying additional makeup with a brush, over that fine work, would obliterate it.

Wrinkles are subject to the same rules of highlight and shadow as bones and cartilage. The deepest parts will be shadowed, and the parts that protrude will be highlighted. Wrinkles are neither symmetrical nor are they regular in width. They may be longer on one side of the face than on the other and they vary in thickness. You may have a wrinkle on one side of the face and not on the other side. Only apply wrinkles where they might actually occur.

To find the placement of wrinkles on your forehead, raise your eyebrows.

Use the sharp end of the smallest flat brush to apply an extremely thin line of shadow in the deepest part of the wrinkle. Alternately apply more and then less pressure as you move along to create a variety of thickness. Make sure your lines are not symmetrical on the face.

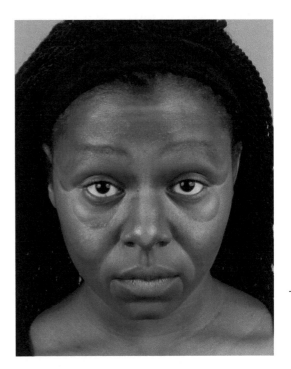

FINDING FOREHEAD WRINKLES

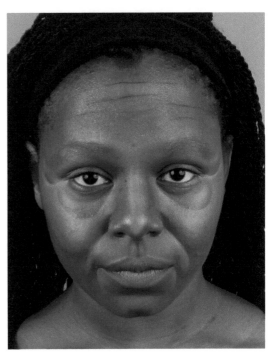

SHADOWING FOREHEAD WRINKLES

Use the flat side of the smallest flat brush to apply highlight to the top of the outward rolls of skin, both above and below the wrinkles.

Because they are so small, you do not need to blend the edges of your highlights and shadows for wrinkles.

To find the placement for wrinkles around your eyes, smile hard, as you would for "apple" cheeks or nasolabial folds or you may need to push up on your cheeks to create wrinkles. When you relax, a trace of the creases will remain.

Notice that the wrinkles start within the eye bag and then curve out over the cheekbone. Apply the shadow and the supporting highlight in the same way as for the forehead wrinkles: thin lines of shadow in the deepest part, highlight on the outward rolls. Because the wrinkles under the eye are so close together, use the sharp end of your brush for the highlights.

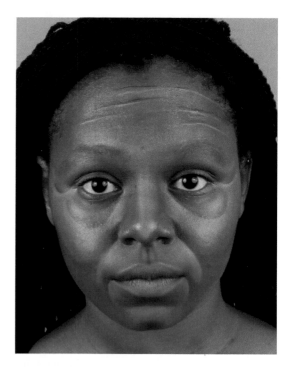

HIGHLIGHTING FOREHEAD WRINKLES

FINDING EYE WRINKLES

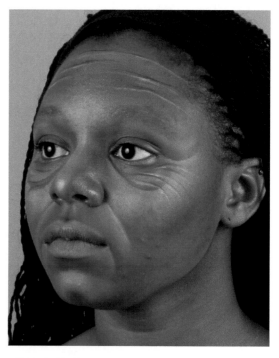

HIGHLIGHTS FOR WRINKLES

Aging the Lips

Apply lip color before adding lines to the lips. Even if your character is wearing lipstick, the lines will show through. Pucker your lips to find the placement of the wrinkles. Notice that the lines are not parallel to each other; rather, they become angled as they move out from the center. Apply the shadow and the supporting highlight following the wrinkles you have made.

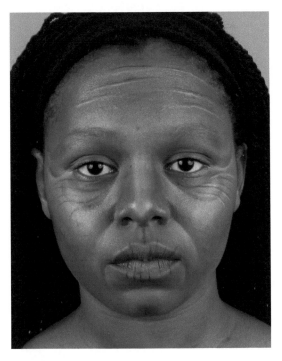

SHADOW IN LIP LINES

SUPPORTING HIGHLIGHT ON LIPS

Stippling

As a result of the aging process, the surface of the skin gets less smooth. The pores get larger, the skin may turn ruddy or develop discoloration from sun damage, and moles may develop. The way to render this with makeup is with a stipple sponge. Stipple sponges are sold cut into cubes; you may round off the hard edges with scissors to avoid unwanted lines of makeup in your application.

Gently press your stipple sponge into your shadow color. Test it on your hand or a paper towel to make sure that you don't have too much makeup on your sponge. Start lightly and work your way darker; you can always add more stipple, but it is next to impossible to remove.

With a light hand, press the stipple sponge against the face, gradually covering the whole of it. Each time you need more makeup on your sponge remember to test it before applying it to your face.

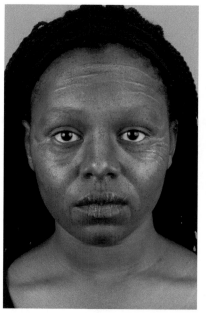

STIPPLED SHADOW ON OLD-AGE MAKEUP

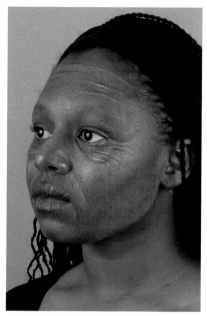

STIPPLED SHADOW OLD-AGE MAKEUP

The final step is powdering, be particularly careful not to disrupt the stippling.

Notice how much the powdering minimizes the highlights and shadows. Take this into consideration when applying makeup.

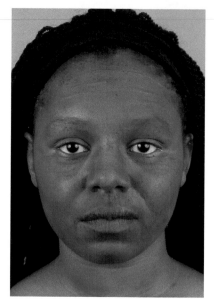

POWDERED OLD-AGE MAKEUP

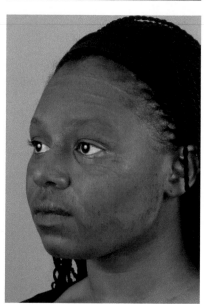

STIPPLING FOR RUDDINESS

If your character has spent a lot of time in the sun (i.e., a farmer, such as Pa Joad in *The Grapes of Wrath*) or perhaps enjoys his ale (i.e., Falstaff or Sir Toby in a play by Shakespeare), you may stipple using a warm, blush color on the cheeks, nose, and forehead.

Using Latex

If you want three-dimensional wrinkles you can apply a very thin layer of clear latex after you have applied your makeup. Stretch the skin on a section of your face and apply the latex, holding the skin taut as it dries. When that section is dry, use a non-latex sponge to apply a thin layer of castor sealer, wipe off as much as possible, then powder. Release the skin and the wrinkles will appear. Work over the entire face in this way.

NOTE: AVOID EYEBROWS, EYELASHES, AND HAIR LINE WHEN USING LATEX. THE LATEX WILL ADHERE PERMANENTLY TO HAIR

STRETCHED SKIN WITH LATEX OVER MAKEUP

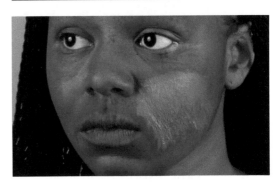

DRIED LATEX WITH CASTOR OIL AND POWDER

Another option is to apply the latex before the makeup. The wrinkles may eliminate the need for much of your age makeup. They will also give you a guide for where to apply highlight and shadow to accentuate the wrinkles.

After applying the castor sealer and powder, carefully apply foundation. Lightly brush highlight onto the latex edges. Last, paint shadow into the creases.

STRETCHED SKIN WITH LATEX ON BARE SKIN

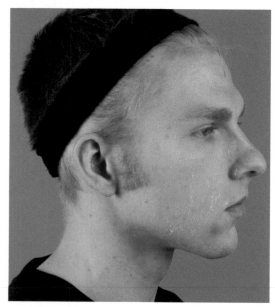

LATEX WITH CASTOR SEALER AND POWDER

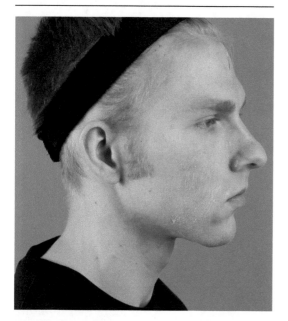

FOUNDATION APPLIED OVER LATEX; HIGHLIGHT BRUSHED ON SKIN FOLDS

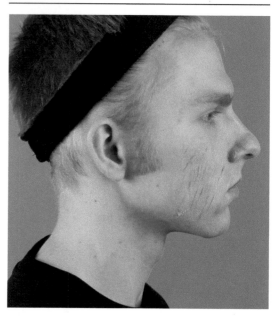

SHADOW IN WRINKLES

Hands

Remember that all of your skin will age. Hopefully your costume designer will have covered up most of your skin, but unless you are wearing gloves you will need to age your hands. Apply base to the top, but not the palms of your hands, blending out the edges. Apply highlight to the individual sections of your fingers and to the knuckles.

Apply shadow in between the knuckles where the fingers join the hand.

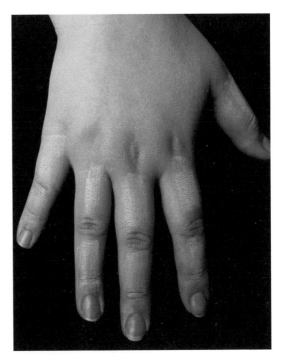

HIGHLIGHTING THE HANDS

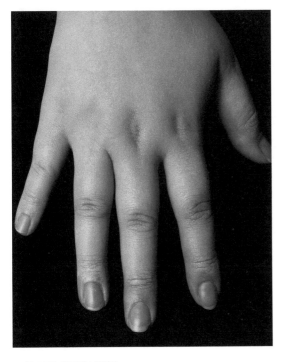

BLENDED HIGHLIGHTS

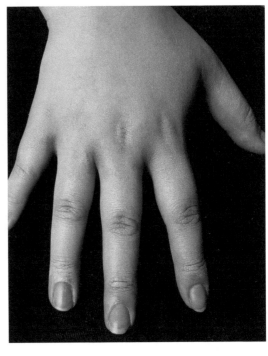

SHADOWING THE HANDS

Flex your hand to create wrinkles in the joints of the fingers. Shadow and highlight the wrinkles as described above in the section on fine lines and wrinkles.

Stipple with a shadow color to replicate age spots and texture.

You can apply latex to the hand by making a fist to stretch the skin. See above in the section on latex.

As discussed above, one may also apply the latex before the makeup. Applying latex and highlight only to the knuckles creates an arthritic look.

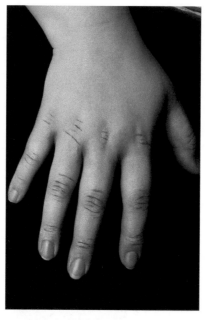

SHADOWED WRINKLES

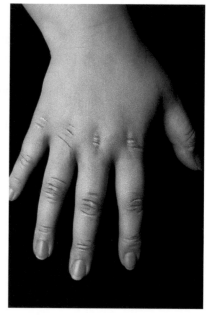

HIGHLIGHTS ON WRINKLES

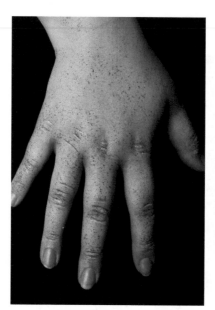

STIPPLED HAND

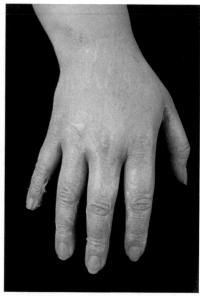

LATEX OVER MAKEUP ON HAND

10

SKIN TEXTURES
AND ABNORMALITIES

As with aging, it is imperative that when you are creating skin textures or abnormalities you do research first, so that you are not "indicating" but truly replicating the look that you want.

Five O'Clock Shadow

Creating the look of a day-or-two-old beard is very simple, but you need to approach it carefully. If you are male, you will know where the outline of your beard and moustache are. If you are a woman playing a man, you will need to do some visual research to determine where the edges should be.

Because natural hair is not all one color, choose two cream colors that are close to your hair color. Even if your hair is black, you will find that is has highlights of a lighter value. Use your stipple sponge as you did in Chapter 9. Starting with the lighter color, carefully press the makeup onto your beard area, a little at a time, fading out towards the edges. Repeat with the darker color, stopping before you get to the edges. If the edge looks a little too regular, you can stipple some base color on it to roughen it up.

Ruddiness, Rosacea, and Acne

Stippling for ruddiness was covered in Chapter 9. Use a warm (reddish) blush cream makeup and carefully stipple onto the cheeks and nose. Rosacea is usually found on the cheeks, nose, and chin. Acne is found anywhere on the face and also on the shoulders and back. You can find many good pictures on the internet. If you skin is light in tone, these conditions are red. If your skin is dark, sometimes these conditions are red, but often they are a purplish color.

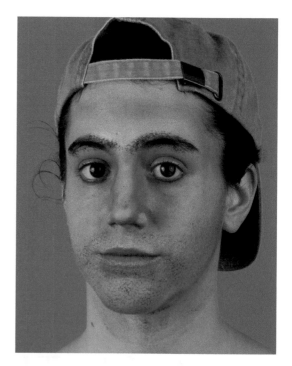

STIPPLED BEARD SHADOW

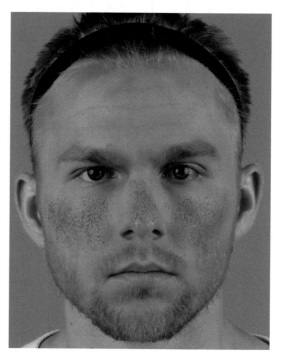

STIPPLED AREA

Start by stippling two shades of red onto the areas you want to cover. For acne, and more extreme forms of rosacea, use the pad of your middle finger to apply additional spots of color. For extreme case of acne, use your finger or a cotton swab to apply dots of a highlight color to the spots.

Finish by stippling cream foundation over the red areas to tone them down.

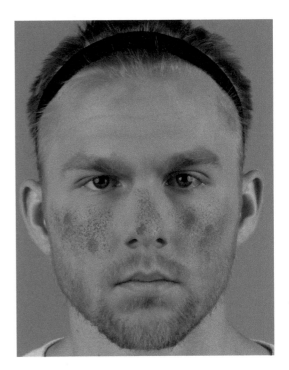

SPOTS

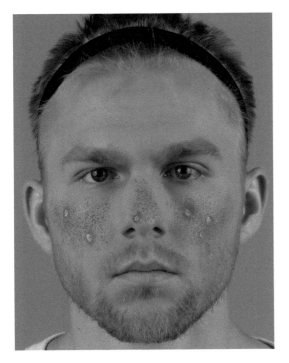

HIGHLIGHTS

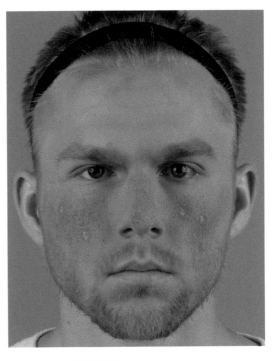

STIPPLED FOUNDATION

Bruises and Black Eyes

Bruises go through a series of stages. They start off dark reddish-purple, turn purplish-black, and then fade back to red, with yellow around the edges as they heal. We will look at these three stages on the eye. Because you will need to use red theatrical makeup near your eyes, test it first when you have time to take care of any reaction. Never use cosmetic lipstick around the eyes because it has oils in it that can irritate and damage your eyes.

For phase one of a black eye, use a stipple sponge to apply a combination of red and purple cream makeup to your eye. When you have a black eye, the blood pools down in the socket, therefore, use more purple in that area, following the curve of the socket.

For phase two of a black eye, use the stipple sponge to apply a combination of purple and

APPLICATION OF RED IN PHASE ONE OF A BLACK EYE

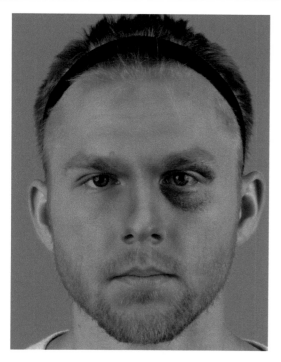

APPLICATION OF PURPLE IN PHASE ONE OF A BLACK EYE

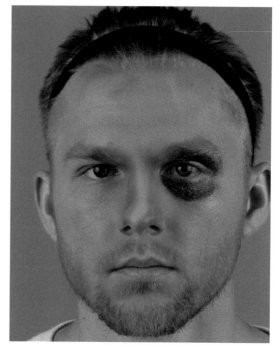

PHASE TWO OF A BLACK EYE

purplish black (mix purple with a little black) cream makeup to the eye socket, again, with the darkest part in the bottom curve of the socket. Use some of the darkest color in the crease of the eye as well.

For phase three of a black eye, begin by applying yellow ochre cream makeup to the eye socket, extending a bit beyond the edges.

Next, apply red to parts of the eye socket.

Finally, apply a small amount of purple just above the edge of the socket and in the crease of the eye.

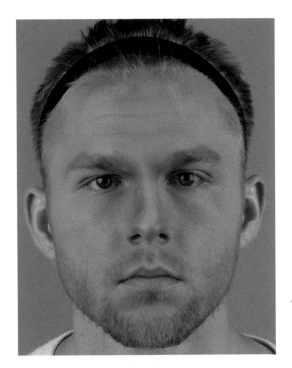

YELLOW BASE OF HEALING BRUISE

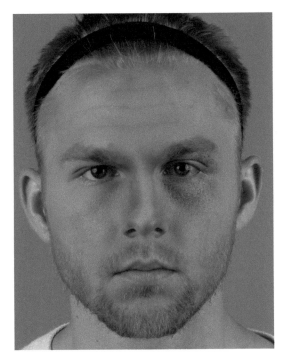

RED LAYER OF HEALING BRUISE

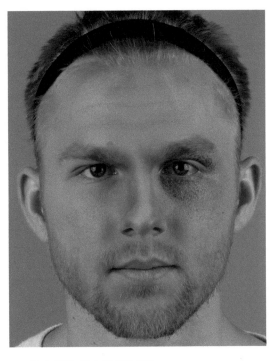

PHASE THREE OF A BLACK EYE

Scars and Welts

Scars and welts are most convincingly created using latex. If you are not allergic to latex you can build your scar directly on your skin. If you are allergic to latex, you can build your scar on a mirror, a piece of glass or a laminate counter, peel it off—powdering the underside as you go and apply it to your face using spirit gum or medical adhesive (see Chapter 11).

Apply a layer of latex to your face a little bit longer and wider than the desired scar. Let the latex dry and repeat two more times. This is the base of your scar.

Unroll a cotton ball and rip off a piece as long as and several times wider than the desired scar. Twist it to the thickness desired; wider in the middle, thinner at the ends. The more irregular your scar is, the more realistic it will look. Cover the twisted cotton with a coat of latex and press it to the latex base on your face.

LATEX BASE OF SCAR

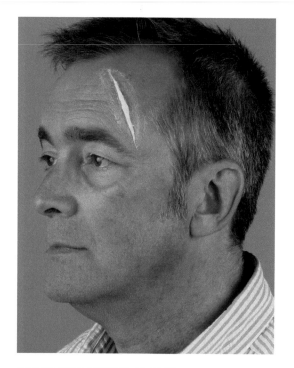

COTTON SCAR ADHERED TO BASE

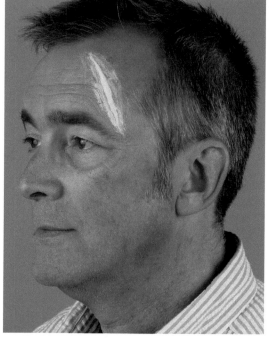

COTTON SCAR COVERED WITH LATEX

Cover the scar with two or three more layers of latex, allowing it to dry between layers.

Use a non-latex sponge to apply a thin layer of castor oil over the scar, wipe off as much as possible, and then powder.

Apply cream foundation to match the rest of your face. Apply highlight to the edge of the scar, then shadow underneath.

If the edge of the scar is too visible, you can soften it by stippling lightly with your shadow color.

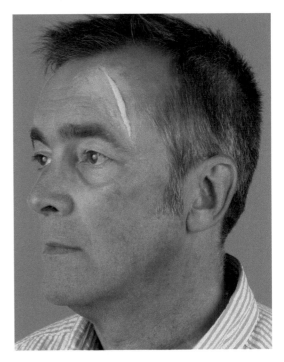

OILED AND POWDERED SCAR

101

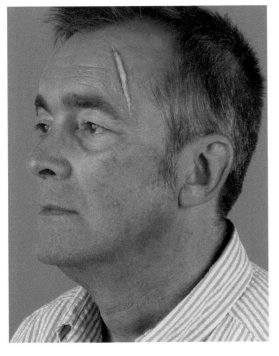

SCAR WITH MAKEUP APPLIED

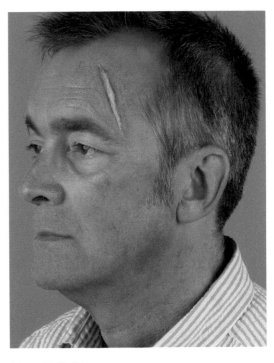

STIPPLED EDGE

Peeling Skin or Sunburn

To create the look of peeling skin, use a single-ply piece of facial tissue or toilet paper and rip it to the size and shape you want. Rip all the way around so there are no even, pre-cut edges.

Apply a layer of latex to your face a little bit larger than the paper.

Let the latex dry and repeat two or three more times.

Before the last layer dries, press the paper to it smoothly so it adheres. Apply three more layers of latex, allowing it to dry each time.

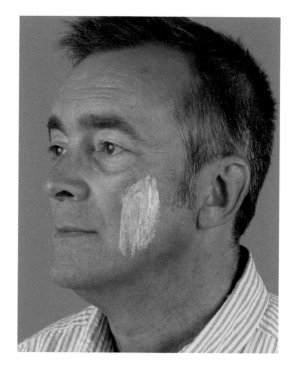

FIRST LAYER OF LATEX

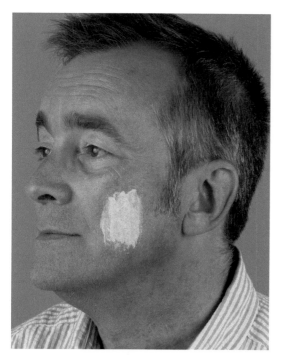

MULTIPLE LAYERS OF LATEX

MULTIPLE LAYERS OF LATEX OVER TISSUE

Use a non-latex sponge to apply a thin layer of castor oil over the "skin." Wipe off as much of the oil as possible, then powder.

Apply cream base to match the rest of your face.

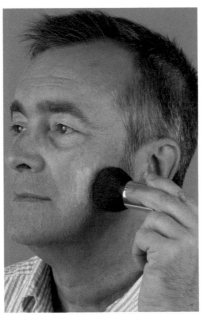

OILED AND POWDERED LATEX "SKIN"

"SKIN" WITH MAKEUP APPLIED

Carefully peel an edge of the latex-coated tissue from your face, powdering the underside.

Apply a reddish color makeup—either cream or powder—to the skin underneath the peeled latex.

PEELING LATEX-AND-TISSUE "SKIN"

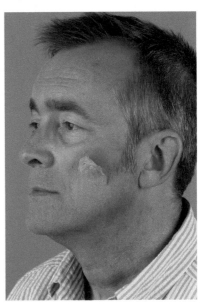

RED MAKEUP SHOWS "TRAUMA"

11

APPLYING FACIAL HAIR AND PROSTHETICS

Because this is a book on basic, not advanced techniques, we will not be covering the actual making of complicated latex prosthetics or facial hair pieces. For those advanced projects I recommend using one of the more all-inclusive texts. If you are performing in a production that requires you to wear false facial hair or a facial prosthetic, it is likely that either the makeup designer or the costume designer will be responsible for providing these; you may or may not be responsible for their application. Pre-made facial hair and latex prosthetics are also readily available to purchase at specialty costume shops and various websites.

There are a number of methods for applying facial hair and prosthetics. For quick application and removal, double-sided toupee tape can be used. Apply the tape to the hair piece first, then to your face. The tape will remove from your face by pulling, usually leaving no residue.

Spirit gum and spirit gum remover are products made specifically for applying and removing facial hair and prosthetics; these items have been staples of makeup kits for many years. Some people are allergic to the ingredients in spirit gum, so many makeup retailers also sell medical adhesive and medical adhesive remover, which seems to be more acceptable to sensitive skin. One may also use a glue stick from an office or crafts store as an application medium. This is a safe and easy option, because it is non-toxic and removes with soap and water.

Applying a Facial Hair Appliance

Before applying a facial hair appliance, wash it with mild soap and water to remove any styling product. Gently press it between the folds of a towel to dry it. When dry, it can be combed. If it has been used previously, carefully remove any remaining adhesive with the appropriate remover.

To apply a facial hair appliance, hold it up to your face to determine exactly where it will sit. Using an eyeliner pencil make a series of dots, about an inch apart, lightly outlining the shape of the piece.

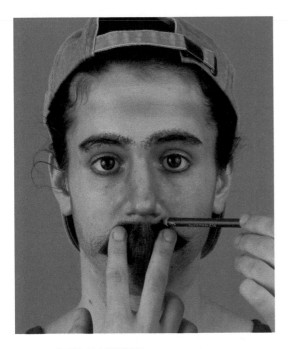

MARKING THE PLACEMENT

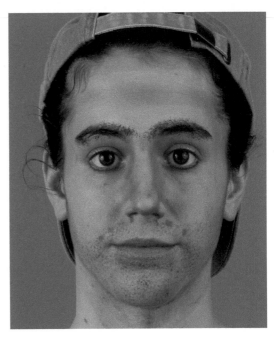

DOTS MARKING PLACEMENT

Next, brush a thin layer of spirit gum or medical adhesive onto your face inside and up to the dots.

Allow the adhesive to dry and get tacky—about a minute. Test it with your finger. Carefully press the piece to your face exactly where you want it. Try to get it right the first time so you don't have to start over.

Using barber shears, trim the hair appliance to the desired shape after it is securely applied.

106

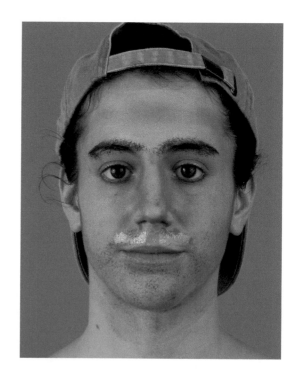

APPLIED ADHESIVE

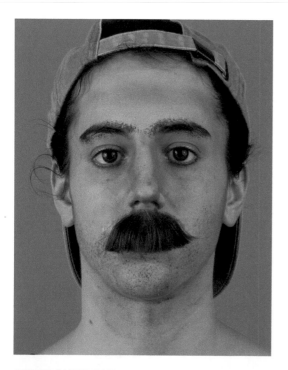

APPLIED FACIAL HAIR

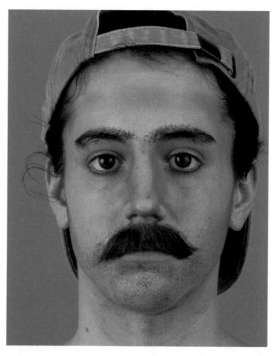

FACIAL HAIR APPLIANCE TRIMMED TO SHAPE

Applying Latex Prosthetics

If a latex prosthetic has been made specifically for you, the makeup artist should already have applied makeup to it. When using a commercial, store-bought facial prosthetic, you will need to apply foundation, highlight, and shadow to coordinate with the makeup on your face. Do this before applying it to your face.

Use the same technique of positioning, marking, gluing, and applying the prosthetic as described above in the section on applying a facial hair appliance.

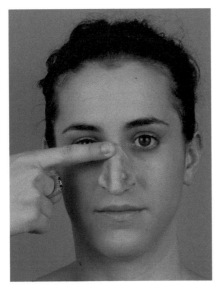

POSITIONING THE PROSTHETIC

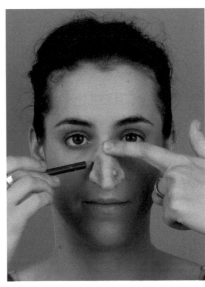

MARKING THE PROSTHETIC

After applying a latex prosthetic, you may need to apply a combination of highlight and shadow with your stipple sponge to diminish to visibility of the edge.

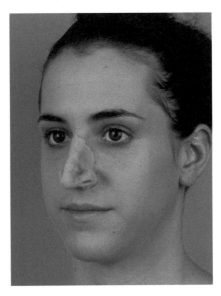

APPLIED LATEX PROSTHETIC

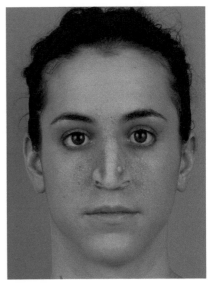

APPLIED LATEX PROSTHETIC WITH STIPPLED EDGE

12

CROSS-GENDER

In previous chapters we have focused on applying natural-looking makeup for your particular, biological gender. There may be times where you will play someone of the opposite gender. This chapter will focus on techniques for looking as much like the opposite gender as possible. It is helpful to have some visual examples to look at.

Women Playing Men

In general (there are exceptions) men tend to have stronger, more squared-off features than women. We will work in strengthening the features.

Often the ridges of the man's forehead will be more prominent and the lower ridge will protrude over the eyes. Sometimes, because of male pattern balding, the forehead will be higher and/or wider. To achieve a more masculine forehead, use the techniques from Chapter 4 to make the forehead higher and wider. Use a little more highlight on the lower ridge to make it appear to protrude more.

NOTE: MEN'S FEATURES TEND TO BE MORE SQUARED-OFF.

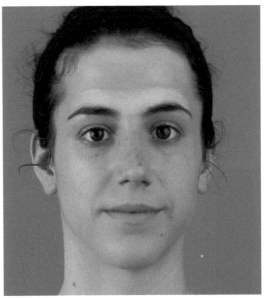

HIGHLIGHT TO HEIGHTEN, WIDEN AND ACCENTUATE FOREHEAD

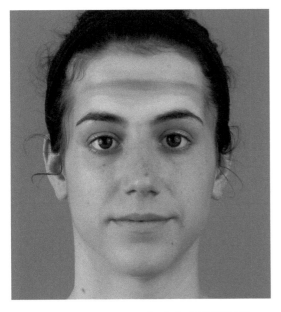

SHADOW TO HEIGHTEN, WIDEN AND ACCENTUATE FOREHEAD

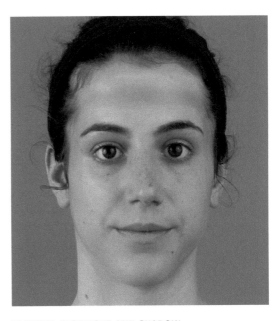

BLENDED HIGHLIGHT AND SHADOW

When applying the shadow, apply it a little darker between the ridges to make the recess look deeper, therefore making the ridges appear more prominent.

To make the lower brow bone appear to overhang the eyes, apply shadow just below it on the bridge of the nose.

To make the nose less feminine, emphasize the center of the bridge by making it wider. Also emphasize the ball of the nose with highlight. Support the highlight with corresponding shadow.

High cheekbones can make a female face look

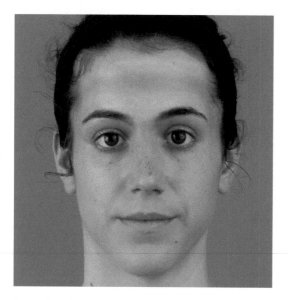

SHADOWING UNDER THE BROW BONE

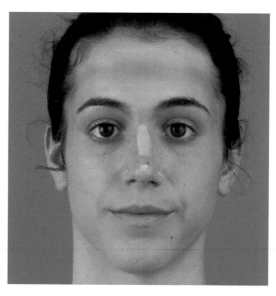

STRENGTHENING THE NOSE WITH HIGHLIGHT

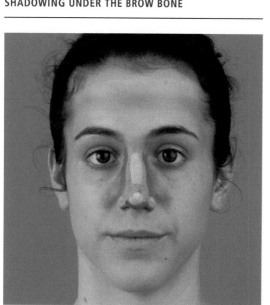

SUPPORTING THE HIGHLIGHTS WITH SHADOW

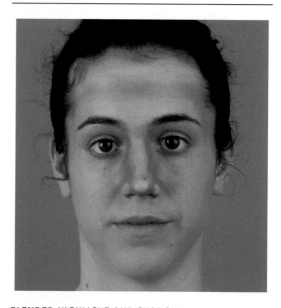

BLENDED HIGHLIGHT AND SHADOW

more feminine. Try lowering the cheekbones by applying the highlight below the vertical, outer plane of the cheekbones.

If your jawline is already very square, emphasize what you have. If it is more rounded, create a square jawline with highlight and shadow.

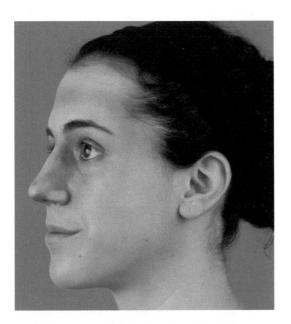

LOWERING THE CHEEKBONES WITH HIGHLIGHT

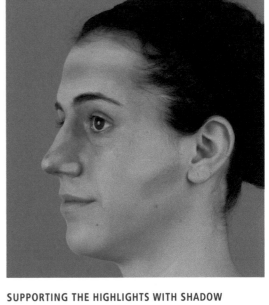

SUPPORTING THE HIGHLIGHTS WITH SHADOW

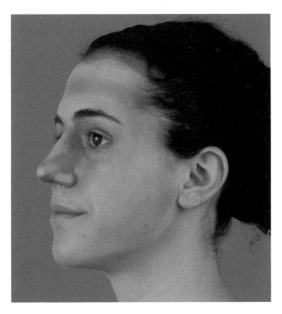

SQUARING OFF THE JAWLINE WITH HIGHLIGHT

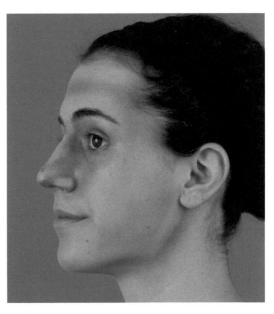

SUPPORTING THE HIGHLIGHTS WITH SHADOW

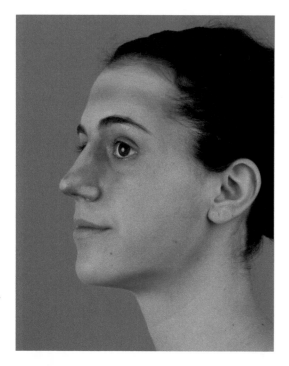

BLENDED HIGHLIGHT AND SHADOW

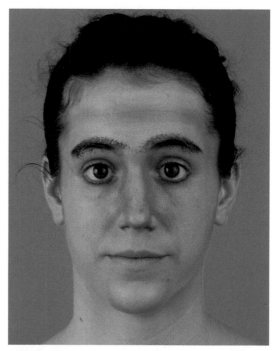

STIPPLED EYEBROWS; LINED LOWER LIDS

To make your eyes less feminine, brush your eyebrows down. If they are very thin or if you have tweezed them you can fill them in by using your stipple sponge either the usual way or by stroking it like a brush. Use eyeliner pencil to line only the lower lid.

Fuller lips tend to look more feminine. Minimize the lips by blocking them out with highlight and then foundation as demonstrated in Chapter 8. Mix a small amount of foundation into your natural lip color and fill in the new, thinner lip shape. Do not use your lip-liner pencil prior to applying lip color.

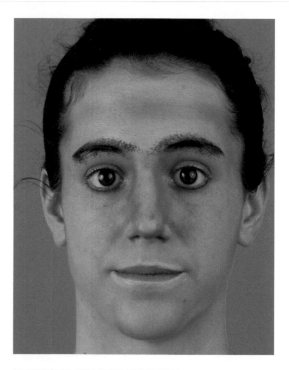

MINIMIZING LIPS WITH HIGHLIGHT

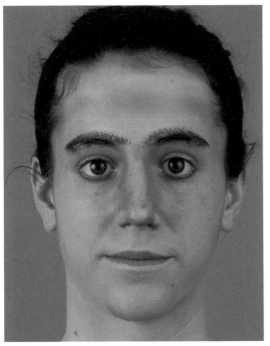

FOUNDATION OVER HIGHLIGHT

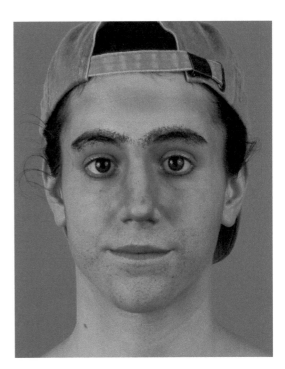

LIGHT STIPPLING ON BEARD AREA

To make the beard area look less smooth, stipple with a cream shadow color a few shades darker than the foundation.

If your character could, conceivably, have a day's growth of beard, use two shades of darker cream shadow to create five o'clock shadow (see Chapter 10).

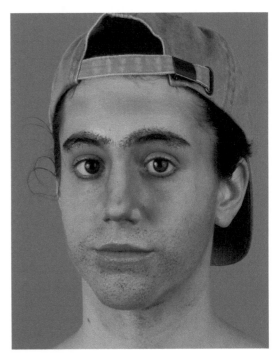

STIPPLED BEARD SHADOW

Men Playing Women

Drag makeup is a very particular style of makeup; it is not what we are doing in this chapter. If you are a man playing a woman, with the intention of the audience believing you are a woman, it is important to keep subtlety at the forefront of your process.

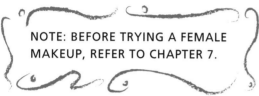

NOTE: BEFORE TRYING A FEMALE MAKEUP, REFER TO CHAPTER 7.

Begin by using concealer and foundation to even out the skin tone and make it appear smoother. You may need to use concealer over the beard area.

If your eyebrows are thick and full you will need to flatten them out before applying the rest of your makeup so you can create a narrow, feminine arch.

EMILIO WITHOUT MAKEUP

AFTER CONCEALER AND FOUNDATION

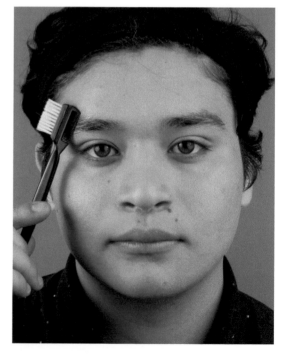

COMBING DOWN THE HAIRS AFTER APPLYING SPIRIT GUM

Brush on spirit gum at the outer end of the eyebrow, pressing down the hairs in the most natural direction (the direction in which they grow). Glue a section at a time and brush the next section over the last, until you have completed as much of the brow as you want. Comb the hairs to press them flat.

NOTE: WOMEN'S FEATURES TEND TO BE MORE DELICATE

Use a non-latex sponge to apply a thin layer of castor sealer over the glued eyebrows, wipe off as much as possible, and then powder.

Another option, demonstrated on the eyebrow on the right, is to use the type of glue stick found in an office supply or craft store. As with the spirit gum, glue down a section at a time, brushing each new section over the last.

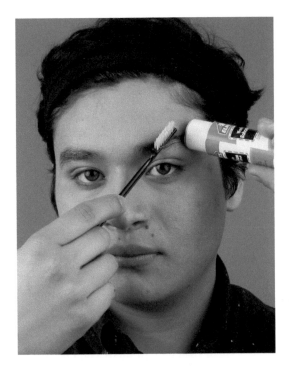

USING A GLUE STICK TO FLATTEN EYEBROWS

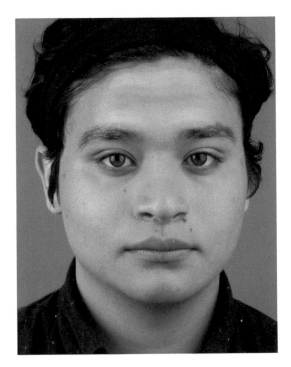

HIGHLIGHT AND SHADOW TO NARROW FOREHEAD AND MINIMIZE BROW

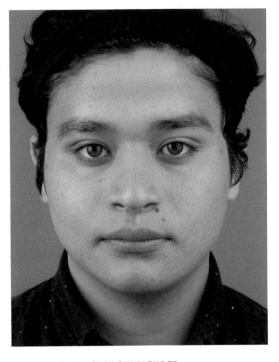

HIGHLIGHT AND SHADOW BLENDED

In general (there are exceptions) women tend to have softer, more delicate features than men. We will work on softening the features.

Women's foreheads tend to be less prominent than men's. If you have very strong brow bones and a large, wide forehead use the techniques from Chapter 4 to make the forehead shorter and narrower. If the lower ridge protrudes over the eyes, move the highlight up a little or, apply highlight only on the outer ends, over the eyebrows, not over the nose. When applying shadow, go a little lighter than usual; this will help to flatten out the forehead.

If you have a very large or wide forehead, discuss the possibility of wearing a hairstyle with bangs, with the costume designer and/or the hair and wig stylist.

To make the nose appear more delicate, use techniques in Chapter 6 to shorten and narrow it.

Accentuate the cheekbones, making them appear higher, as demonstrated in Chapter 6.

HIGHLIGHT AND SHADOW TO NARROW AND SHORTEN NOSE

HIGHLIGHT AND SHADOW BLENDED

HIGHLIGHT AND SHADOW TO HEIGHTEN CHEEKBONES

Use the techniques from Chapter 4 to soften and round out the jawline. Bring the shadow up onto the corner of the jawline to support the highlight.

SQUARE JAWLINE BEFORE MAKEUP

HIGHLIGHT AND SHADOW TO SOFTEN JAWLINE

HIGHLIGHT AND SHADOW BLENDED

Now you can apply highlight and shadow to contour the eyes. Refer to the section on defining the eyes for women in Chapter 5.

If your eyebrows are dark you will need to use a very light highlight over the glued-down area to conceal them.

If your upper eyelids are not completely covered by your brow bone or upper lid, apply eyeliner. If your lids are small or obscured, line the lower lid. When applying eyeliner to the upper lid, holding the lashes of one eye down helps you keep your other eye open. When applying eyeliner to the lower lid, tilt your head down and look up at the mirror.

Use the side of the eyeliner pencil to darken the new eyebrow line.

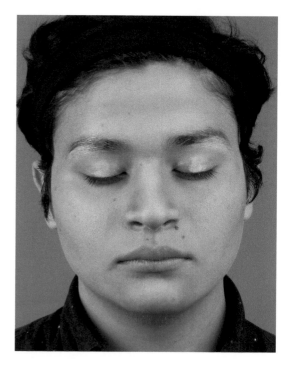

HIGHLIGHT ON BROW AND LID

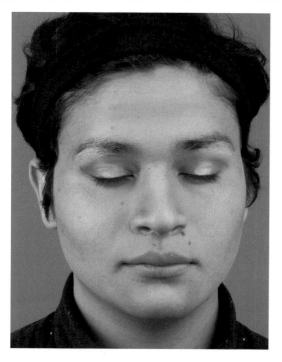

SHADOW IN CREASE

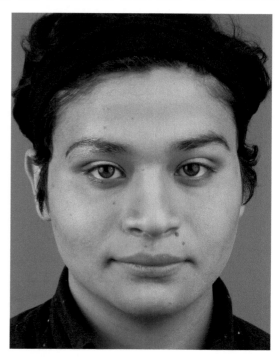

BLENDED

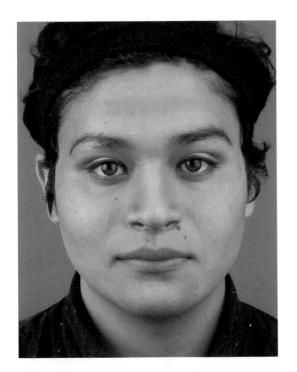

CONTOURED AND DEFINED FEMININE EYE

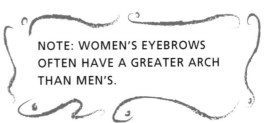

Apply mascara. Apply blush (powder or cream) horizontally on the cheekbone. Use a lip-lining pencil to create a fuller outline of the lips. It helps to start with a dot at each of the upper points and on the lower point at the center of the upper lip.

Connect the dots and continue lining the rest of the lips. Try for a full, yet natural shape. Use your medium or small flat brush to blend the inside of the pencil line inwards, leaving the outer edge sharp.

119

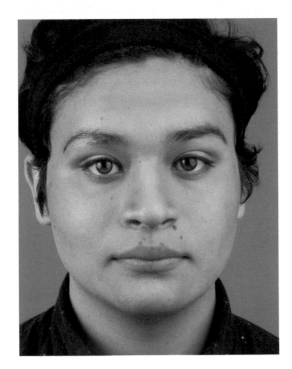

DOTS OF LIP-LINER

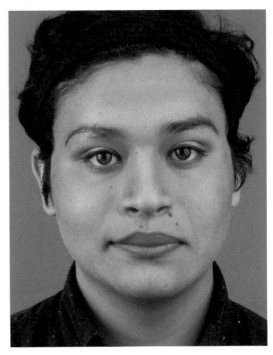

LINING THE LIPS

Use your medium or small flat brush to pick up
some cream lip color and fill in the lines.

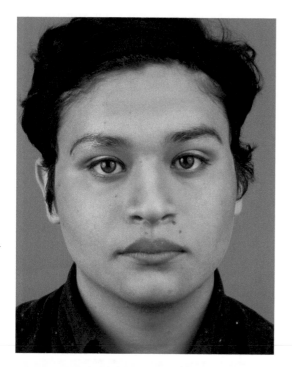

BLENDING THE LIP LINE INWARDS

FINISHED LIP COLOR

13

HISTORICAL PERIOD AND THEATRICALIZED MAKEUP

Just as each era had its own styles in fashion and clothing, it also had its individual style in makeup. Much of the time this affected only the women of the period, but in a few cases in the past men have also worn makeup. In theatre, certain genres in different eras have utilized their own particular style of makeup. In these cases, both men and women (if the women were permitted on the stage) wore theatrical makeup.

When creating a period or theatrical makeup, thoroughly research the art and fashion of the time before you begin. This chapter is meant as a starting point and, as such, the explanations are simplified. We will look at a selection of western (mostly European) makeup styles that you might be called upon to apply. In most cases before the twentieth century, makeup was worn only by the wealthy upper classes and those in high society, therefore it was geared towards Caucasian skin tones. Each case of "nontraditional casting" deserves its own serious discussion between the actor, director, and designers to determine how the makeup will be approached. In the twentieth century we will look at glamorous, high-style makeup made popular by movie stars and models of a variety of ethnicities.

If the production you are in has a makeup designer, you will follow her or his design and instructions. Sometimes the costume designer is responsible for makeup choices and you will defer to him or her. If you have neither, make sure your makeup style is consistent with that of the rest of the cast.

Ancient Egypt

The artwork of ancient Egypt shows a focus on thick, dark lining of the eyes and the eyebrows for both men and women. The lines are often extended beyond the natural shape of the eye. Skin often has a warm, reddish tone. Lips are a natural shape and often colored terracotta. Basic contouring of the features would be a good base to start from. Use black liner pencil on the eyes and eyebrows. In this case you can draw the eyebrows in rather than just coloring the hairs.

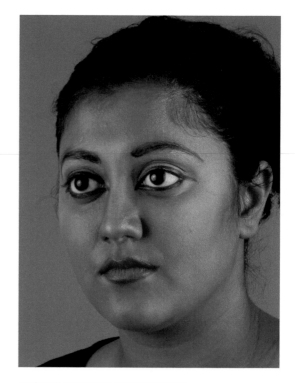

ANCIENT EGYPTIAN MAKEUP STYLE

NOTE: IT IS IMPORTANT TO DO RESEARCH AND HAVE VISUAL REFERENCES WHEN APPLYING HISTORICAL MAKEUP.

Classical (Greek and Roman)

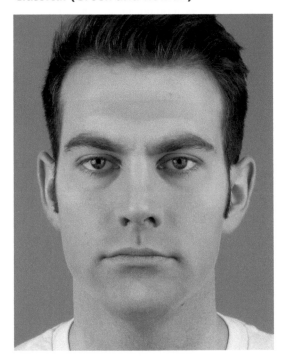 

HIGHLIGHTS FOR A SCULPTED, CLASSICAL EFFECT

During the classical period only men appeared on the stage, and they wore masks. When a classical Greek or Roman play is performed now, the desire is sometimes for the actors (both men and women) to look somewhat like the sculpture of the period. The features are strong and symmetrical; they may look squared-off and seem almost carved from marble.

To achieve this look, use highlight to straighten and lengthen the nose, connecting it to the lower ridge of the forehead. Cheekbones will be high and the jawline will be rounded but deep.

Place the shadows closer to the highlights than usual. This will leave a smaller area for blending, creating a harder, more chiseled edge. Darken the shadows at the deepest points, creating a stronger contrast between the highlights and shadows.

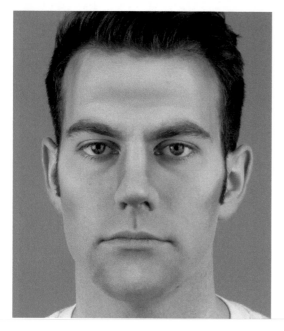
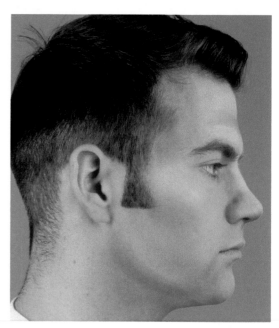

SHADOWS FOR A SCULPTED, CLASSICAL EFFECT

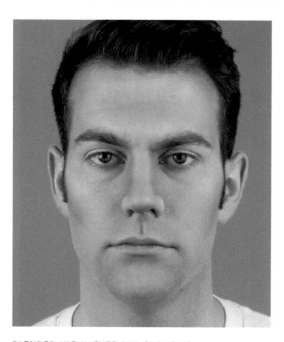

BLENDED HIGHLIGHTS AND SHADOWS

Another characteristic of the sculpture of this period is full, defined lips on both men and women. Create the shape first with a lip-liner pencil, blending it inward. Then fill in the outline with a natural lip color.

DEFINED LIPS

Gothic

During the fourteenth and fifteenth centuries in Europe, especially northern Europe in the Burgundian region, it was popular for upper-class women to have pale skin, a very high, plucked forehead, and minimal eyebrows. Jan van Eyck's 1432 painting, *Giovanni and Giovanna Arnolfini* provides a good example.

Choose a lighter-than-usual base color (unless you already use a light base). Use the technique demonstrated in Chapter 6 to create a high forehead. If your eyebrows are thick, you may need to use spirit gum to glue them down as demonstrated in the section on men playing women in Chapter 12. If your eyebrows are dark, apply cream highlight to lighten them. Apply your theatrical base over the highlight on your eyebrows. Stipple highlight and shadow above and below your eyebrows to visually break up the skin surface, and minimize the difference between it and the texture of the eyebrows.

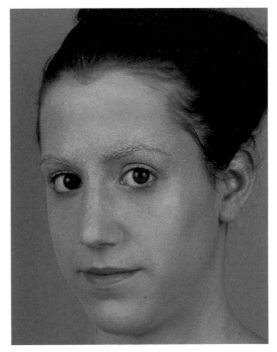

GOTHIC MAKEUP STYLE

Renaissance

Men and women during this period had a very natural look. A basic corrective makeup would work for most plays set during this time.

Elizabethan/Shakespearean

Women did not appear on stage until King Charles II was restored to the English throne in 1660. Prior to this, young men dressed and made up as women, played the women's roles in the plays of Shakespeare and his contemporaries. High foreheads and pale skin remained popular with upper-class women through the Elizabethan period. During this era, paleness was so prized that women's skin was often made up to appear as white as milk. In contrast to this whiteness, rouge was painted on the lips in a small, bow shape. Eyebrows were minimal, but visible. Near the end of the period (after 1600) rouge was also applied to the cheeks. The many paintings of

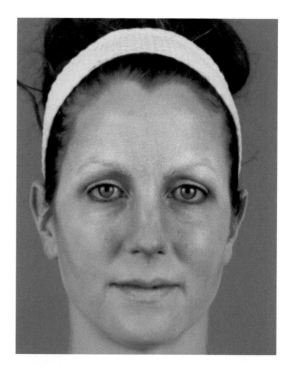

SHADOWS TO CONTOUR

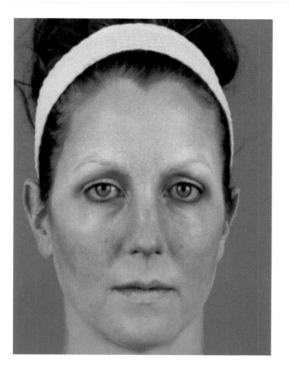

BLUSH

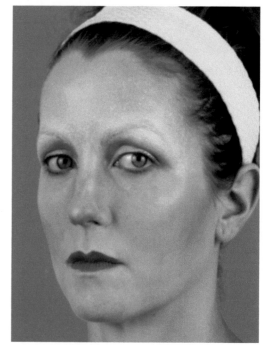

ELIZABETHAN MAKEUP

Queen Elizabeth I of England demonstrate this style.

Use a very pale base with some white mixed in. If your eyebrows are thick, you can use the base/white mixture to block out the area you want to hide. Use a light shade of brown or tan for shadow contouring. Highlight is not necessary, or even possible, because your base is so light.

Use a pink or coral shade of red for blush.

Use a lip pencil to outline the lips and blend the lines inward as described in Chapter 5. Fill in the lips with the same color used on your cheeks.

Men of the Elizabethan period were also relatively pale, compared to today. Very fashionable men of the upper classes might wear makeup to make their skin paler for court, or when sitting for a portrait. Carefully trimmed beards (which came to a point) and moustaches (often curved upwards) were very popular, as were carefully groomed and arched eyebrows. The miniatures of Nicholas Hilliard, especially the portrait of the Earl of Essex, are good examples of this style.

Restoration

Both male and female actors in early Restoration theatre of the late seventeenth century wore makeup. Very light or white skin was still popular as were lip paint and cheek rouge. The cheek rouge tended to be focused on the center of the cheek. The lips were still bow-shaped. Women's eyebrows were more visible than in the past and carefully shaped into a gentle arch like the men's. Face patches (small pieces of black velvet cut into dots, hearts, crescents, and other shapes) were used to hide blemishes. Nell Gwynne and Thomas Betterton were popular actors in this era.

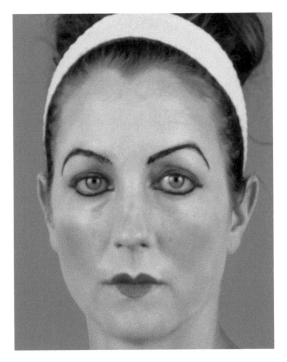

FEMALE RESTORATION MAKEUP

MALE RESTORATION MAKEUP

Eighteenth Century

By the eighteenth century, men returned to a more natural look. Women remained pale, but not white. Soft, pink rouge was used on the center of the cheeks and on the lips. Eyebrows looked natural. The paintings of Antoine Watteau and William Hogarth beautifully represent the style of the day.

Nineteenth Century

For most of the nineteenth century, women looked natural. A basic corrective makeup would work for most plays set during this time.

Turn of the Twentieth Century

In the late 1890s and into the early 1900s the "Gibson Girl" look was in style. Named for the illustrations of Charles Dan Gibson, the feminine ideal was natural, with strong, classical features. Squared-off eyebrows were popular. Lips were full and bowed.

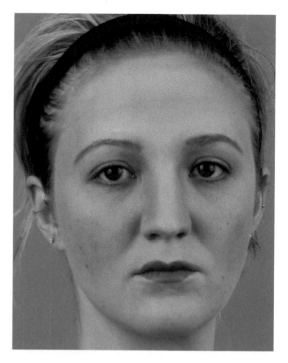

EIGHTEENTH-CENTURY MAKEUP STYLE

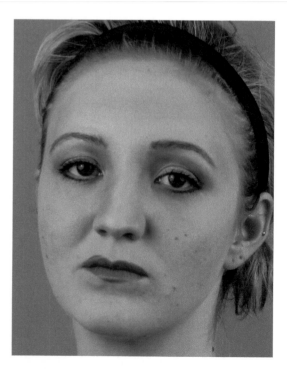

GIBSON GIRL MAKEUP STYLE

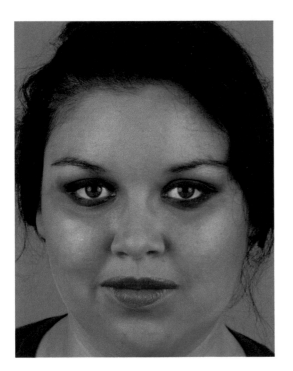

1920S MAKEUP STYLE

The 1920s

During the 1920s the focus was on the eyes. Upper and lower lids were thickly lined and often blended out for a "smoky" look. Performers such as Josephine Baker and Louise Brooks drew the outer ends of their eyebrows into a straight line. Lips were dark and full, often glossy.

The 1930s

In the 1930s women tweezed their eyebrows into a high, curved arch. Sometimes they tweezed the entire brow and drew a new one above it in imitation of the actresses Jean Harlow, Anna May Wong, and Marlene Dietrich. Eyelids and the orbital part were often neutral (skin tone) or might be contoured with shadow in the crease. Long, starry false eyelashes were the rage. Lips were red and bow-shaped.

129

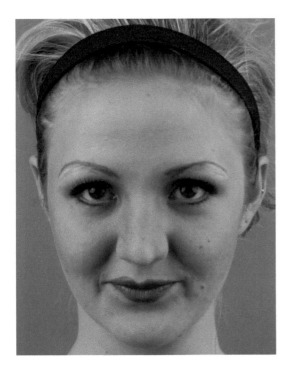

1930S MAKEUP STYLE

1940s

During the war years women grew back their eyebrows but kept them neatly groomed. Eyelids were contoured; lashes were still full, but not quite as spiky. Joan Crawford, Bette Davis, and other stars of the day squared off the top lip by filling in the space above the top edge at the corners. The overall look had a strength befitting Rosie the Riveter.

1950s–early 1960s

Women in the 1950s and early 1960s copied the style of movie stars Marilyn Monroe and Elizabeth Taylor and TV star Diahann Carroll. The "cat eye" was popular along with a contoured lid and a dark, arched brow. Lips were full and bright in the 1950s, paler in the early 1960s.

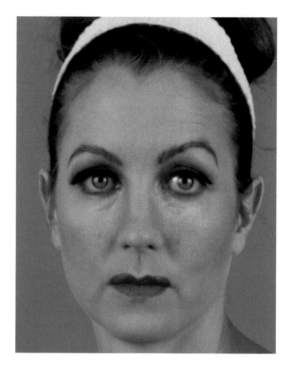

1940S MAKEUP STYLE

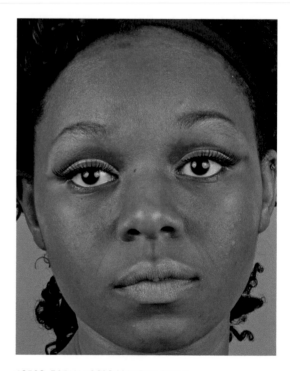

1950S–EARLY 1960S MAKEUP STYLE

MID-1960S MAKEUP STYLE

Mid-1960s

By the mid-1960s models Jean Shrimpton and Twiggy had helped to glamourize a youthful look of dramatically contoured eyes and pouty, pale lips. Lashes could be even more full or spiky than in the 1930s.

1970s

During the disco years dark, glittery eye-shadow, plucked eyebrows, bold blush, and bright lip gloss were worn by women emulating the look of Donna Summer, Cher, and other disco divas.

1970S DISCO MAKEUP STYLE

1980s

Whether you were a "good girl" like Brooke Shields, or a "downtown girl" like Madonna or Cyndi Lauper, in the 1980s you had thick, dark eyebrows. While Brooke and wannabe members of the Breakfast Club might sport minimal makeup, the girls who wanted to have fun used thick eyeliner, smoky eye-shadow, and neon colors on their lips.

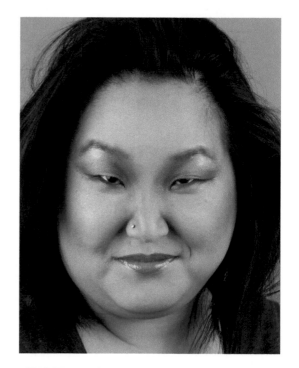

1980S MAKEUP STYLE

14

MAKEUP
WORKSHEETS

In academic makeup classes, many instructors require their students to create makeup worksheets before class to use as a guide when applying their makeup in class. The makeup worksheet is a very useful pedagogical tool because it helps the student think about the process of makeup design and it helps them plan his or her makeup application.

The makeup worksheet can also be a useful tool for the amateur or professional actor. If you are going to be applying a corrective makeup, and you are well-practiced at that, you may not need a worksheet. But if you are using makeup in any other way—for example, to create the appearance of age, or to manipulate bone structure or cartilage—you may want to make notes on a worksheet beforehand. If you are performing in a production in which your makeup has been designed for you, the designer may either teach you how to apply your makeup while you take

notes on a makeup worksheet, or they may have already created the worksheet for you.

There are several different types of worksheets. There are pre-made worksheets provided by manufacturers of cosmetics and some you can find in other makeup textbooks or from theatrical makeup manufacturers. While these are convenient, they are only moderately helpful. The major problem with a pre-made worksheet is that the shape and proportions of the face and features are "one-size-fits-all," but never really fit anyone. It is much more beneficial, and accurate, to make your own personal worksheet using a photo of your own face. It is also relatively easy.

Start by having two pictures taken of your face; one from the front and one from the side. Your hair should be pulled off of your face (use a headband if necessary) and you should not be wearing any makeup.

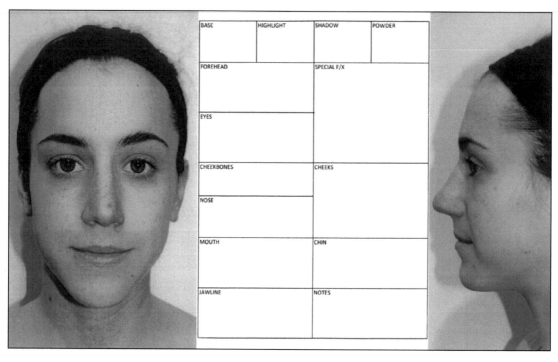

MAKEUP WORKSHEET

Generate an instruction grid that includes the following section titles:

Base	Highlight	Shadow
Powder	Forehead	Eyes
Cheekbones	Cheeks	Nose
Mouth	Jawline	Chin
Notes	Special F/X	

Put the instruction grid together with your front and side view facial photos. You can either do this all on the computer or, if you are not very tech-savvy (like me) you can use glue or tape. Print or photocopy several so you will have them handy when needed.

Now you are ready to draw the makeup design on the worksheet. For this example I will be creating an old age (75) makeup for a 25-year-old actress. The first thing I will do is collect visual research of women within that age range and within the same ethnic group (Caucasian). In particular I will look at pictures of both her maternal and paternal grandmothers taken when they were in their seventies.

VISUAL RESEARCH

Once you have your research, you can use pencils in the colors of your base, highlight, and shadow to render the design onto your photo. Doing this is almost exactly like applying makeup to your face—just follow the directions in the earlier chapters. If you can apply makeup, you can render your design on your worksheet.

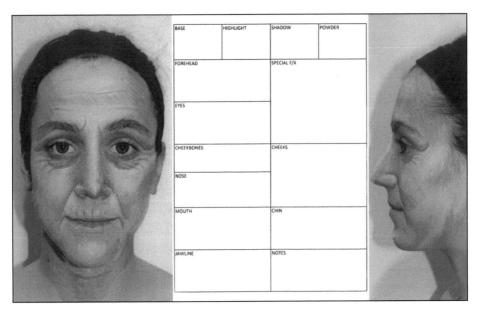

MAKEUP RENDERING ON PHOTO

The next step—one that I use with my students to help them translate from rendering to application—is to cover your rendering with tracing paper and draw what I call the road map. The road map is a plan of the application of the makeup. It shows the shape and placement of each swath of makeup as well as showing which edges are blended out and which remain hard. It is very helpful in reminding you where to leave room between your highlight and shadow (most places) and where to place them side-by-side (nasolabial folds, etc.)

While you are drawing your road map, write your application instructions in the instruction grid.

If you are skilled with technology you can do this whole process on the computer.

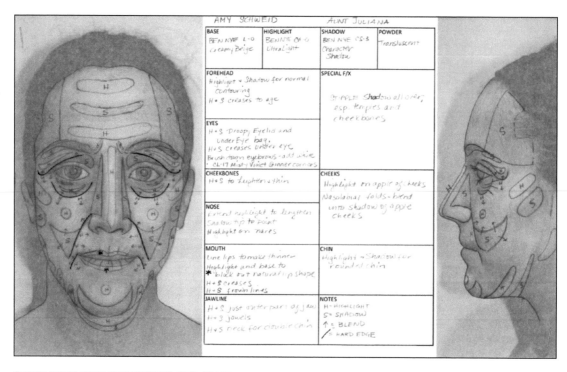

"ROAD MAP" WITH INSTRUCTION GRID FILLED IN

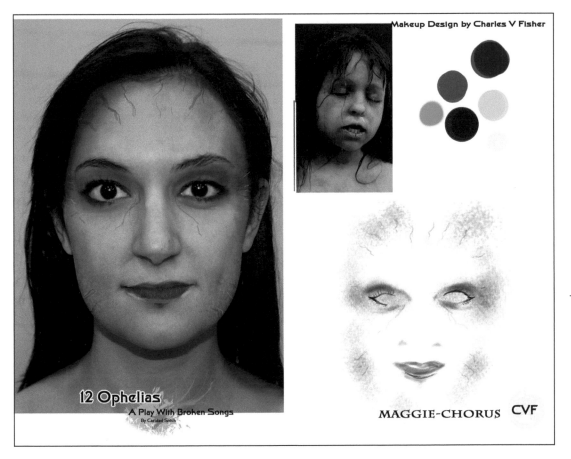

Makeup Design by Charles V Fisher

12 Ophelias
A Play With Broken Songs
By Caridad Svich

MAGGIE-CHORUS CVF

MAKEUP DESIGN BY CHARLES V. FISHER

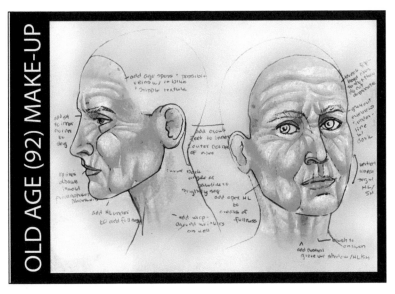

OLD AGE (92) MAKE-UP

MAKEUP DESIGN BY MALLORY MARIA PRUCHA

Figures are shown in *italics*.